KEY
A Railway
B Grand Canal
C Ca' Capello, Rio Marin
D S. Cassiano
E Rialto
F Palazzo Rezzonico
G Frari
H Accademia
I Palazzo Barbaro
J Ca' Alvisi
K Hotel Barbesi
L S. Maria della Salute
M Stabilimento Chitarin
N Giudecca Canal
O Piazza S. Marco
P Doges' Palace
Q Café Orientale
R 4161 Riva degli Schiavoni
S S. Giorgio Maggiore
T Casa Jankovitz
U Rio Panada
V Murano

THE VENETIAN HOURS
of
HENRY JAMES, WHISTLER AND SARGENT

For Michael Mallon

Whistler, Venetian Scene, 1879-80

First United States Edition
First published by Walker Books Ltd, 87 Vauxhall Walk, London SE11 5HJ

ISBN 0-8212-1861-1

Library of Congress Catalog Card Number 91-70163
Library of Congress Cataloging-in-Publication information is available.

Bulfinch Press is an imprint and trademark of Little, Brown and Company (Inc.)
Published simultaneously in Canada by Little, Brown and Company
(Canada) Limited

PRINTED IN HONG KONG

THE VENETIAN HOURS

of

HENRY JAMES, WHISTLER AND SARGENT

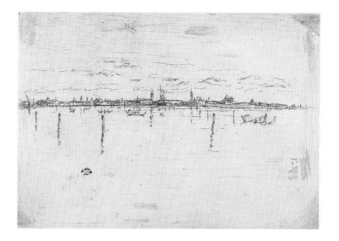

Hugh Honour & John Fleming

A Bulfinch Press Book

Little, Brown and Company

Boston • Toronto • London

CONTENTS

ACKNOWLEDGEMENTS

For permission to reproduce paintings, drawings, prints, pastels and photographs we thank most warmly their private owners (many of whom wish to remain anonymous) as well as the custodians of public collections mentioned in the List of Illustrations.

Passages from Henry James's letters are reprinted by permission of the publisher from *Henry James: Selected Letters*, Leon Edel, editor, Cambridge, Mass.: The Belknap Press of Harvard University Press, Copyright © 1975, 1975, 1980, 1984, 1987 Leon Edel, Editor, and Copyright © 1974, 1975, 1980, 1984, 1987 Alexander R. James copyright material; and from *The Letters of Henry James*; Leon Edel, Editor, Cambridge, Mass.: The Belknap Press of Harvard University Press, Copyright © 1984 by Leon Edel, Editor, and Copyright © 1984 by Alexander R. James. All rights reserved. And with permission of Macmillans as regards British Commonwealth Rights.

A passage from Henry James's notebooks is reprinted by permission of the publisher from *The Complete Notebooks of Henry James*; Leon Edel and Lyall H. Powers, editors, Oxford University Press, New York; Copyright © 1987.

PREFACE

The idea for this book came to us some years ago at Asolo, north of Venice, in a house which Henry James knew well. It still belongs to the family of his great Venetian friend, Mrs Bronson, and her presence and that of James himself can be felt there, lingering, as they had so often, to watch the evening light glow across the great plain towards Venice and the sea. However, the idea might never have been realized had not our friend and publisher Sebastian Walker given us the opportunity. We are extremely grateful to him. While preparing the book we have incurred many other debts of gratitude to old friends and also to several new friends that this book has brought us and it is a great pleasure to acknowledge them all here. In connection with Henry James we are indebted to Leon Edel, Michael Mallon and Rosella Mamoli Zorzi; also to Arthur J. Rosenthal and Beth Kiley of Harvard University Press as regards material still in copyright. Margaret F. MacDonald was unstinting with her help concerning Whistler and also lent us many photographs; Richard Ormond and Odile Duff were similarly generous with their knowledge concerning Sargent and in lending photographs. For information about Mrs Bronson and Ca' Alvisi we are much indebted to her grandaughter, Marchesa Nannina Fossi, and to several of her other descendants especially dott. Maria Fossi-Todorow, Giovanna Rucellai Piqué and Conte Eugenio Rucellai; for information about James's Venetian friends, the Curtises, we are indebted to Patricia Curtis-Viganò who welcomed us to Palazzo Barbaro which remains, incredibly, just as James knew and loved it a hundred years ago. Many other friends have helped and we should particularly like to thank Professor Alessandro Bettagno, Bruce Boucher, Charles Cholmondeley, Dr François Daulte, Karen Haas, Professor Francis Haskell, Phillip Kelley, Katherine A. Lochnan, H. P. Naud, Christopher Noey, Gill Ravenal, Joseph Rishell, Professor Giuseppe Pavanello, Professor John Shearman, Robert Silvers, Nikos Stangos, the Hon. James Stourton, Carl Strehlke, Denys Sutton and Dr Italo Zannier. At Walker Books we are greatly indebted to Wendy Boase and David Ford, and the book owes a very great deal to Jim Bunker's skill as a designer.

Hugh Honour   John Fleming
December 1989

First Impressions: Henry James

"The simplest thing to tell you of Venice is that I adore it – have fallen deeply and desperately in love with it," wrote Henry James on 12th June 1881.[1] "I had been there twice before but each time only for a few days. This time I have drunk deep, and the magic potion has entered my blood." He was nearing the end of one of the longest of his many visits to the city which he loved above all others but from which he always, in the end, reluctantly withdrew. Like his passionate friendships, it was the object of a devotion that was never allowed to become too intimate. He toyed more than once with the idea of renting there a *pied-à-terre* or "foot-in-the-water", as he called it, to which he might at any time escape – "treating it, cherishing it as a sort of repository of consolations" – for he had found in Venice something that no other place could give. He had friends and acquaintances who took small one-room or two-room apartments in Venice at about this time. But James never did. He abandoned the idea – for want of cash, he said – and came no closer to making any permanent arrangement than he did to marrying. Nevertheless, for more than thirty years he went on returning, both physically and in his imagination, recalling and evoking the Venetian atmosphere in countless letters and essays as well as more allusively in his fiction. The genius of the place has a haunting presence in his work, more obsessively so than in that of the only other contemporary writers of comparable gifts, Marcel Proust and Thomas Mann, who fell victim to the city's lulling but potent spell and tried to exorcise it in their writing.

Carlo Naya, San Giorgio Maggiore, c.1875

During these same years Venice was depicted by two artists, both of whom, like James, were expatriate Americans. John Singer Sargent, who came for the first time as an eighteen-year-old youth with his parents in 1874, returned in 1880 to paint the first of a hundred or so Venetian scenes and subjects which he did during his later, almost annual visits, up to 1913. In September 1879

Edmond Behles,
The Salute, c.1870
(a stereoscopic photograph)

James McNeill Whistler arrived. It was his first and only visit, but he stayed much longer than intended, putting off and putting off his departure, until the middle of the following November. He had to write several times to his dealers in London and beg for further loans of money so that he could prolong his stay. And Whistler's year in Venice was to mark an epoch in his art as well as in his life.

It was in Venice that Whistler met Sargent for the first time. Both knew Katherine De Kay Bronson and the Curtises, Americans then living in the city, who were also friends of Henry James. James, of course, had met both Whistler and Sargent in London. But what links the two artists with the writer is not so much the social web as the affinity of their responses to the city – to its elegiac evanescence, its fading opulence and pervasive odour of decay – highly individual responses, which distinguish their work from that of all other artists who painted Venice at this time, even that of such great painters as Manet, Renoir and Monet[2] or that of the gifted, eccentric American, Maurice Prendergast. For Renoir and Monet, Venice was still, as it had been for Turner, the Venice of Canaletto and Guardi. They painted the same celebrated views – in full summer sunlight, the variously coloured marble façades shimmering across the wide expanse of the lagoon. They showed no interest in exploring the city's unfrequented canals and *campi* – unlike Whistler and Sargent who discovered what James had also found, a "Venice in Venice" that no one else had known.

Carlo Naya,
The Grand Canal,
c.1868

Henry James was the first of the three to be rowed down the Grand Canal, aged twenty-six and still at the beginning of his career. That was in 1869. Three years earlier Venice had been surrendered by the Austrians and incorporated into Italy, by then all but completely united. Venetians had been groaning under, and plotting to free themselves from, the Austrian yoke ever since it had been imposed on them in 1815. They had risen and fallen heroically in 1848. But in the complicated intrigues and equivocal war

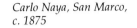

Carlo Naya, San Marco,
c. 1875

of 1866 which preceded the cession of the Veneto to the Kingdom of Italy, they played virtually no part: it was all arranged by Napoleon III, Wilhelm I of Prussia, Franz Josef of Austria and, as a gesture of courtesy between crowned heads, Victor Emanuel of Savoy, despite the ignominious defeat of both his army and his navy by the Austrians. "Liberation" was thus something of an anti-climax. It was to 1848 rather than to 1866 that Venetians were to look back with pride. But many patriots returned to Venice in 1866 from their forced or voluntary exile to live again in their damp, dilapidated family homes. The Italian tricolour replaced the Austrian banners on the great flag-posts in front of St Mark's in the piazza. Soldiers lounging there and along the waterfront wore Italian uniforms and not the dandy white coats of Austria. Otherwise, there were very few changes. Venice remained as impoverished as it had been ever since Trieste was developed as the sea-port of the Austro-Hungarian empire. Tourism suffered a set-back after the political upheavals and was slow in recovering. Little progress was made in the revival of the glass industry, still occupied mainly in the production of souvenirs. There was, on the other hand, a fortunate pause in the work of urban "improvement" begun under the Austrians – the spanning of some small canals with iron bridges and the filling in of others to make streets, not to mention the harsh restoration of ancient monuments about which Ruskin had been so vociferous.

When he went sightseeing on this first visit, James was guided by books written some years earlier. On the recommendation of Charles Eliot Norton, the professor of fine art at Harvard, he consulted the "Venetian Index", a kind of gazetteer, in the third volume of Ruskin's *The Stones of Venice*, published in 1853. Also like most English visitors of the time, he used Murray's *Handbook for Travellers in Northern Italy*, first published in 1842, little altered in its edition of 1869 except in its practical information and some expansions to take account of Ruskin's "discovery" of Tintoretto. And he seems to have had with him Théophile Gautier's more evocative than informative travel book of 1852, *Italia*, some two-thirds of which is devoted to Venice. He must surely also have read, before leaving America, William Dean Howells' *Venetian Life*, published in 1867, and including several essays previously printed in the *Boston Advertiser*. Howells had been the American consul in Venice from 1861 to 1865 and his book presents a vivid account of the city in those years, one that is generally happy despite references to Austrian oppression. Concerned with the living inhabitants more than with the stones of Venice, it was critical of Ruskin in a way that may well have influenced James. "Ruskin is undoubtedly the best guide you can have in your study of the Venetian painters," Howells wrote, "and after reading him, and suffering confusion and ignominy from his theories and egotisms, the exercises by which you are chastised into admitting that he has taught you anything cannot fail to end in a humility very favourable to your future as a Christian. But even in this subdued state you must distrust the methods by which he pretends to relate the aesthetic truths you perceive to certain civil and religious conditions…"[3] When Howells returned to America, settled in Cambridge and became assistant editor of the *Atlantic Monthly* in 1866, he struck up a long and lasting friendship with James, whose literary abilities he was quick to recognize on the basis, at that time, of only a few published short stories.

Just as much as other visitors to Venice, James was well prepared in advance for what he was to see, not only by Ruskin and Gautier and Howells but by the innumerable writers from Shakespeare to Byron, Mme de Staël, Fenimore

Cooper and George Sand, who had created the "myth" of Venice. "Venice is quite the Venice of one's dreams," he told his painter friend John La Farge a week after arriving in 1869, "but it remains strangely the Venice of dreams, more than of any appreciable reality. The mind is bothered with a constant sense of the exceptional character of the city; you can't quite reconcile it with common civilization. It's awfully sad too in its inexorable decay."[4]

In August James had crossed the Simplon Pass on foot with "an individual" to carry his knapsack, then he went by diligence "down, down – on, on into Italy – a rapturous progress thro' a wild luxuriance of corn and frescoed villages and clamorous beggars and all the good old Italianisms of tradition."[5] After halts at Milan, Pavia, Brescia, Verona and Vicenza, he reached Venice on about 14th September and took a room at the Hotel Barbesi, the first among those recommended in the current (1869) Murray's *Handbook*: "Hôtel Barbesi in the Pal. Zucchelli, on the Grand Canal, opposite the ch. of La Salute, in a quiet situation, many of the apartments looking S. 2 minutes walk from the Piazza di S. Marco. Arrangements during a prolonged stay may be made advantageously for board and lodging at the H. Barbesi, which has a garden on the canal with a southern aspect, a fine view over the Lagunes, and in a good situation; as a winter residence it is comfortable in every respect: the proprietor speaks English; table-d'hôte at $4\frac{1}{2}$ frs. without wine: bedrooms 2 to 5: breakfast 1.50 to 2. Baths in the house."[6]

James spent the next fortnight wandering round the city. By the 21st he was able to tell La Farge: "I have seen a vast number of paintings, palaces and churches and received far more 'impressions' than I know what to do with. One needs a companion to help him dispose of this troublesome baggage."[7] To his brother William he wrote at greater length on 25th and 26th September about everything he had seen: "If I could only write as I might talk I should have no end of things to tell you about my last days in Switzerland, and

Carlo Naya, Visiting the Doges' Palace, c.1870

especially my descent of the Alps – that mighty summer's day upon the Simplon when I communed with immensity and sniffed Italy from afar. This Italian tone of things which I then detected, lies richly on my soul and gathers increasing weight, but it lies as a cold and foreign mass – never to be absorbed and appropriated. The meaning of this superb image is that I feel I shall never look at Italy – at Venice, for instance – but from without; whereas it seemed to me at Oxford and in England generally that I was breathing the air of home. Ruskin recommends the traveller to frequent and linger in a certain glorious room at the Ducal Palace, where Paolo Veronese revels on the ceilings and Tintoret rages on the walls, because he 'nowhere else will enter so deeply into the heart of Venice.' But I feel as if I might sit there forever (as I sat there a long time this morning) and only feel more and more my inexorable Yankeehood."[8]

He then went on to enlarge, for several pages, on the Venetian painters, following Ruskin in the emphasis he placed on Tintoretto, Veronese and Jacopo Bellini – especially Tintoretto for whom, he said, "there is nothing for me to do but admit (and have done with it) to be the biggest genius (as far as I yet know) who ever wielded a brush." Titian he "gave up", even the great *Assumption* in the Frari striking him "as a magnificent second-rate picture". In these and many other comments and descriptions of Venetian paintings that he sent his brother, Ruskin might have been whispering into one ear and Gautier into the other. It must surely have been Ruskin who led him to such an out-of-the-way church as San Cassiano,[9] for example, with its three Tintorettos; elsewhere it was more often Gautier who, as it were, showed him the way and sometimes James's comments echo almost word for word what Gautier had said. In the Sala del Collegio of the Doges' Palace he simply resumed Gautier's gasping, amoral dithyramb in front of Veronese's *Rape of Europa* – "where a great rosy blond, gorgeous with brocade and pearls and bouncing with salubrity and a great mellow splendor of sea and sky and nymphs and flowers do their best to demoralize the world into a herd of Théophile Gautiers."[10] For, in his heart, James had less sympathy with the sternly dogmatic Ruskin than with the hedonist author of *Mademoiselle de Maupin* and *Emaux et camées*. With Gautier to reassure and encourage him he could temporarily put aside, if not quite suppress, his Puritan misgivings about the sultry, lush opulence of Venice and Venetian art.

*Antonio Bianchi, Visitors to
the Doges' Palace, c.1870*

By the time he left the whole Venetian scene and atmosphere, its extraordinary combination of past splendour and present squalor had fired his imagination without, as yet, unduly disturbing him with its social and moral implications. "Decay is in this extraordinary place golden in tint and misery *couleur de rose*," he was to write later and it was this ambivalence that he found so alluring and that was to go on fascinating him. "Everyone knows that the Grand Canal is a wonder" but really to feel and understand and appreciate Venice it was essential to have seen "the number and splendor of the palaces that stand rotting and crumbling and abandoned to paupers." The miserable, impoverished Venetians he found "immensely picturesque", though squalid and "offensive to the nostrils". But from the far side of a canal and in bright sunshine "to light them up as they go pushing and paddling and screaming – bare-chested, bare-legged, magnificently tanned and muscular – the men at least are a very effective lot." He watched them appreciatively while "lolling in my gondola". He also spent "a good deal of time in poking about the *campos* – the little squares formed about every church – some of them most sunnily desolate, the most grass-grown, the most cheerfully sad little reliquaries of a splendid past that you can imagine."

However, writing from Florence on 6th October, James began to feel slightly uneasy about his first impressions of Venice. Already, he told his sister Alice, Venice seemed

Carlo Naya, The Giudecca, c.1875

"a figment of the past – she lies like a great dazzling spot of yellow paint upon the backward path of my destiny. Now that I behold her no more I feel sadly as if I had done her wrong – as if I had been cold and insensible – that with more self-oblivion I might have known her better and loved her more. Wherever we go we carry this heavy burden of our personal consciousness and wherever we step we open it out over our heads like a great baleful cotton umbrella, to obstruct the prospect and obscure the light of heaven.

"Apparently it is in the nature of things. To come away vaguely dissatisfied with my Venetian sojourn is only one chapter in the lesson which this hardened old Europe is forever teaching – that you must rest content with the flimsiest knowledge of her treasures and the most superficial insight into her character. I feel sadly the lack of that intellectual outfit which is needful for seeing Italy properly and speaking of her in words which shall be more than empty sounds – the lack of facts of all sorts – chiefly historical and architectural. A mind unprepared by the infusion of a certain amount of knowledge of this kind, languishes so beneath the weight of its impressions, light as they might necessarily be – that it is ready to give up the game as lost. Your only consolation is in the hope that you may be able by hook or by crook to retain a few of the impressions and confront them with the facts in the leisure of subsequent years."[11]

Within twelve months he had worked up his first impressions of Venice into a short story, *Travelling Companions*, published in the *Atlantic Monthly* for November-December 1870.[12] The narrator follows James's route from Milan by way of Vicenza to Venice with Murray's guidebook in hand: "The day succeeding my arrival I spent in a restless fever of curiosity and delight, now lost in the sensuous ease of my gondola, now lingering in charmed devotion before a canvas of Tintoretto or Paul Veronese. I exhausted three gondoliers and saw all Venice in a passionate fury and haste. I wished to probe its fulness and learn at once the best – or the worst.

"'Well,'" he asks the heroine, Miss Evans, when he meets her again in Venice, "'What has Venice done for you?'

"'Many things. Tired me a little, saddened me, charmed me.'

"'How have you spent your time?'

"'As people spend it… You must have learned already how sweet it is to lean back under the awning, to feel beneath you that steady, liquid lapse, to look out at all this bright, sad elegance of ruin.'"

In the following pages there are few descriptions of the paintings about which he had written to his brother William, apart from the Tintorettos in San Cassiano; he concentrated on evoking the narrator's general response: "Late in the afternoon I disembarked at the Piazzetta and took my way haltingly and gazingly to the many-domed Basilica, – that shell of silver with a lining of marble. It was that enchanting Venetian hour when the ocean-touching sun sits melting to death, and the whole still air seems to glow with the soft effusion of his golden substance. Within the church, the deep brown shadow-masses, the heavy thick-tinted air, the gorgeous composite darkness, reigned in richer, quainter, more fantastic gloom than my feeble pen can reproduce the likeness of. From those rude concavities of dome and semi-dome, where the multitudinous facets of pictorial mosaic shimmer and twinkle in their own dull brightness; from the vast antiquity of innumerable marbles, incrusting the walls in roughly mated slabs, cracked and polished and triple-tinted with eternal service; from the wavy carpet of compacted stone, where a thousand once-bright fragments glimmer through the long attrition of idle feet and devoted knees; from sombre gold and mellow alabaster, from porphyry and malachite, from long dead crystal and the sparkle of undying lamps, – there proceeds a dense rich atmosphere of splendor and sanctity which transports the half-stupefied traveller to the age of a simpler and more awful faith. I wandered for half an hour beneath those reverted cups of scintillating darkness, stumbling on the great stony swells of the pavement as I gazed upward at the long mosaic saints who curve gigantically with the curves of dome and ceiling. I had left Europe; I was in the East. An overwhelming sense of the sadness of man's spiritual history took possession of my heart. The clustering picturesque shadows about me seemed to represent the darkness of a past from which he had slowly and painfully struggled. The great mosaic images, hideous, grotesque, inhuman, glimmered like the cruel spectres of early superstitions and terrors. There came over me, too, a poignant conviction of the ludicrous folly of the idle spirit of travel. How with Murray and an opera-glass it strolls and stares where omniscient angels stand diffident and sad! How blunted and stupid are its senses! How trivial and stupefied its imaginings! To this builded sepulchre of trembling hope and dread, this monument of mighty passions, I had wandered in search of pictorial effects. O vulgarity! Of course I remained, nevertheless, still curious of effects."

James never wrote a more purple passage – one reason, no doubt, why he was to exclude *Travelling Companions* with its simple plot from the New York edition of his works. In this immature but nonetheless appealing series of *impressions de voyage*, strung on the slender thread of a youthful romance, there are many other atmospheric evocations of Venice in the evening light and by night – the clear light of day seldom shining, for James, on this city of fallen splendour. The companions of the title are rowed across the lagoon "in a golden silence which suffered us to hear the far-off ripple in the wake of other gondolas, a golden clearness so perfect that the rosy flush on the marble palaces seemed as light and pure as the life-blood on the forehead of a sleeping child. There is no Venice like the Venice of that magical hour. For that brief period her ancient glory returns. The sky arches over her like a vast imperial canopy crowded with its clustering mysteries of light. Her whole aspect is one of unspotted splendor. No other city takes the crimson evanescence of day with such magnificent effect. The lagoon is sheeted with a carpet of fire. All torpid, pallid hues of marble are transmuted to a golden glow. The dead Venetian tone brightens and quickens into life and lustre, and the spectator's enchanted vision seems to rest on an embodied dream of the great painter who wrought his immortal reveries into the ceilings of the Ducal Palace."

When darkness falls Venice becomes more animated: "After dinner we went down to the Piazza and established ourselves at one of Florian's tables. Night had become perfect; the music was magnificent. At a neighboring table was a group of young Venetian gentlemen, splendid in dress, after the manner of their kind, and glorious with the wondrous physical glory of the Italian race. 'They need only velvet and satin and plumes,' I said, 'to be subjects for Titian and Paul Veronese.' They sat rolling their dark eyes and kissing their white hands at passing friends, with smiles that were like moon-flashes on the Adriatic." By a curious coincidence, a Neapolitan artist, Michele Cammarano, painted just such a scene in the year of James's visit, 1869. But the description of Venetian sunsets suggests the pastels that Whistler was to paint a decade later.

James returned to Venice briefly, accompanying his sister Alice, on 2nd September 1872. From mosquitoes they "suffered such nightly martyrdom as even Venice was hardly a good enough cause to make endurable", he told their parents.[13] "The curtains pompously affixed to the beds were a mockery and a delusion, and the only way to attain sleep was to burn certain stifling pastilles within the net to woo oblivion while the ravenous beasts were temporarily stupefied. This of course was not wholesome in the long run, and the great heat (from which our first week in Italy was entirely free, and which overtook us only at Venice) did not make it more so." They stayed only four days. "Most delightful days they were, for it was only the nights that were obnoxious. We left nothing unseen that we wished to see, lived in our gondola, and found abundant coolness on the water and in the darksome churches. We went to Torcello – an ever memorable excursion; to Murano; twice to the Lido (which has been sadly 'improved' since I was there last) but where we dined most breezily on a platform where bathers and diners were strewn in true Italian promiscuity; spent much time in St Mark's, and had ample leisure to see all the desirable pictures. The weather was perfect, we ate innumerable

Michele Cammarano,
Evening in Piazza San
Marco, 1869

figs, ices every night at Florian's and bought a few very beautiful photographs (all of pictures, many of which you have not seen) ..." In retrospect the excursion to Torcello, where he had not been before, was to stand out "in a sort of supernatural relief. We had two mighty gondoliers, and we clove the wandering breezes of the lagoon, like a cargo of deities descending from Olympus. Such a bath of light and air – color and general luxury, physical and intellectual!"

Despite the brevity of the visit, James had time to prepare, perhaps also to write, the first of his essays on Venice,[14] which was published in *The Nation* on 6th March 1873:

There would be much to say about that golden chain of historic cities which stretches from Milan to Venice, in which the very names – Brescia, Verona, Mantua, Padua – are an ornament to one's phrase; but I should have to draw upon recollections now three years old and to make my short story a long one. Of Verona and Venice only have I recent impressions, and even to these I must do hasty justice. I came into Venice, just as I had done before, toward the end of a summer's day, when the shadows begin to lengthen and the light to glow, and found that the attendant sensations bore repetition remarkably well. There was the same last intolerable delay at Mestre, just before your first glimpse of the lagoon confirms the already distinct sea-smell which has added speed to the precursive flight of your imagination; then the liquid level, edged afar off by its band of undiscriminated domes and spires, soon distinguished and proclaimed, however, as excited and contentious heads multiply at the windows of the train; then your long rumble on the immense white railway-bridge, which, in spite of the invidious contrast drawn, and very properly, by Mr Ruskin between the old and the new approach, does truly, in a manner, shine across the green lap of the lagoon like a mighty causeway of marble; then the plunge into the station, which would be exactly similar to every other plunge save for one little fact – that the keynote of the great medley of voices borne back from the exit is not 'Cab, sir!' but 'Barca, signore!'
I do not mean, however, to follow the traveller through every phase of his initiation, at the risk of stamping poor Venice beyond

repair as the supreme bugbear of literature; though for my own part I hold that to a fine healthy romantic appetite the subject can't be too diffusely treated. Meeting in the Piazza on the evening of my arrival a young American painter who told me that he had been spending the summer just where I found him, I could have assaulted him for very envy. He was painting forsooth the interior of St Mark's. To be a young American painter unperplexed by the mocking, elusive soul of things and satisfied with their wholesome light-bathed surface and shape; keen of eye; fond of colour, of sea and sky and anything that may chance between them; of old lace and old brocade and old furniture (even when made to order) of time-mellowed harmonies on nameless canvases and happy contours in cheap old engravings; to spend one's mornings in still, productive analysis of the clustered shadows of the Basilica, one's afternoons anywhere, in church or *campo*, on canal or lagoon, and one's evenings in starlight gossip at Florian's, feeling the sea-breeze throb languidly between the two great pillars of the Piazzetta and over the low black domes of the church – this, I consider, is to be as happy as is consistent with the preservation of reason.

The mere use of one's eyes in Venice is happiness enough, and generous observers find it hard to keep an account of their profits in this line. Everything the attention touches holds it, keeps playing with it – thanks to some inscrutable flattery of the atmosphere. Your brown-skinned, white-shirted gondolier, twisting himself in the light, seems to you, as you lie at contemplation beneath your awning, a perpetual symbol of Venetian 'effect'. The light here is in fact a mighty magician and, with all respect to Titian, Veronese and Tintoret, the greatest artist of them all. You should see in places the material with which it deals – slimy brick, marble battered and befouled, rags, dirt, decay. Sea and sky seem to meet half-way, to blend their tones into a soft iridescence, a lustrous compound of wave and cloud and a hundred nameless local reflections, and then to fling the clear tissue against every object of vision. You may see these elements at work everywhere, but to see them in their intensity you should choose the finest day in the month and have yourself rowed far away across the lagoon to Torcello. Without making this excursion you can hardly pretend to know Venice or to sympathize with that longing for pure radiance which animated her great colourists. It is a perfect bath of light, and I couldn't get rid of a fancy that we were cleaving the upper atmosphere on some hurrying cloud-skiff. At Torcello there is nothing but the light to see – nothing at least but a sort of blooming sand-bar intersected by a single narrow creek which does duty as a canal and occupied by a meagre cluster of huts the dwellings apparently of market-gardeners and fishermen, and by a ruinous church of the eleventh century. It is impossible to imagine a more penetrating case of unheeded collapse. Torcello was the mother-city of Venice, and she lies there now, a mere mouldering vestige, like a group of weather-bleached parental bones left impiously unburied. I stopped my gondola at the mouth of the shallow inlet and walked along the grass beside a hedge to the low-browed, crumbling cathedral. The charm of certain vacant grassy spaces, in Italy, overfrowned by masses of brickwork that are honeycombed by the suns of centuries, is something that I hereby renounce once and for all the attempt to express; but you may be sure that whenever I mention such a spot enchantment lurks in it.

A delicious stillness covered the little *campo* at Torcello; I remember none so subtly audible save that of the Roman Campagna. There was no life but the visible tremor of the brilliant air and the cries of half-a-dozen young children who dogged our steps and clamoured for coppers. These children, by the way, were the handsomest little brats in the world, and each was furnished with a pair of eyes that could only have signified the protest of nature against the meanness of fortune. They were very nearly as naked as savages, and their little bellies protruded like those of infant cannibals in the illustrations of books of travel; but as they scampered and sprawled in the soft, thick grass,

Naya studio, Torcello canal, c.1870

grinning like suddenly-translated cherubs and showing their hungry little teeth, they suggested forcibly that the best assurance of happiness in this world is to be found in the maximum of innocence and the minimum of wealth. One small urchin – framed, if ever a child was, to be the joy of an aristocratic mamma – was the most expressively beautiful creature I had ever looked upon. He had a smile to make Correggio sigh in his grave; and yet here he was running wild among the sea-stunted bushes, on the lonely margin of a decaying world, in prelude to how blank or to how dark a destiny? Verily nature is still at odds with propriety; though indeed if they ever really pull together I fear nature will quite lose her distinction. An infant citizen of our own republic, straight-haired, pale-eyed and freckled, duly darned and catechised, marching into a New England schoolhouse, is an object often seen and soon forgotten; but I think I shall always remember with infinite tender conjecture, as the years roll by, this little unlettered Eros of the Adriatic strand. Yet all youthful things at Torcello were not cheerful, for the poor lad who brought us the key of the cathedral was shaking with an ague, and his melancholy presence seemed to point the moral of forsaken nave and choir. The church, admirably primitive and curious, reminded me of the two or three oldest churches of Rome – St Clement and St Agnes. The interior is rich in grimly mystical mosaics of the twelfth century and the patchwork of precious fragments in the pavement not inferior to that of St Mark's. But the terribly distinct Apostles are ranged against their dead gold backgrounds as stiffly as grenadiers presenting arms – intensely personal sentinels of a personal Deity. Their stony

Naya studio, Torcello, c.1870

stare seems to wait forever vainly for some visible revival of primitive orthodoxy, and one may well wonder whether it finds much beguilement in idly-gazing troops of Western heretics – passionless even in their heresy.

I had been curious to see whether in the galleries and temples of Venice I should be disposed to transpose my old estimates – to burn what I had adored and adore what I had burned. It is a sad truth that one can stand in the Ducal Palace for the first time but once, with the deliciously ponderous sense of that particular half-hour's being an era in one's mental history; but I had the satisfaction of finding at least – a great comfort in a short stay – that none of my early memories were likely to change places and that I could take up my admirations where I had left them. I still found Carpaccio delightful, Veronese magnificent, Titian supremely beautiful and Tintoret scarce to be appraised. I repaired immediately to the little church of San Cassano, which contains the smaller of Tintoret's two great Crucifixions; and when I had looked at it awhile I drew a long breath and felt I could now face any other picture in Venice with proper self-possession. It seemed to me I had advanced to the uttermost limit of painting; that beyond this another art – inspired poetry – begins, and that Bellini, Veronese, Giorgione, and Titian, all joining hands and straining every muscle of their genius, reach forward not so far but that they leave a visible space in which Tintoret alone is master. I well remember the exaltations to which he lifted me when first I learned to know him; but the glow of that comparatively youthful amazement is dead, and with it, I fear, that confident vivacity of phrase of which, in trying to utter my impressions, I felt less the magniloquence than the impotence. In his power there are many weak spots, mysterious lapses and fitful intermissions; but when the list of his faults is complete he still remains to me the most interesting of painters. His reputation rests chiefly on a more superficial sort of merit – his energy, his unsurpassed productivity, his being, as Théophile Gautier says, *le roi des fougueux.*

These qualities are immense, but the great source of his impressiveness is that his indefatigable hand never drew a line that was not, as one may say, a moral line. No painter ever had such breadth and such depth; and even Titian, beside him, scarce figures as more than a great decorative artist. Mr Ruskin, whose eloquence in dealing with the great Venetians sometimes outruns his discretion, is fond of speaking even of Veronese as a painter of deep spiritual intentions. This, it seems to me, is pushing matters too far, and the author of *The Rape of Europa* is, pictorially speaking, no greater casuist than any other genius of supreme good taste. Titian was assuredly a mighty poet, but Tintoret – well, Tintoret was almost a prophet. Before his greatest works you are conscious of a sudden evaporation of old doubts and dilemmas, and the eternal problem of the conflict between idealism and realism dies the most natural of deaths. In his genius the problem is practically solved; the alternatives are so harmoniously interfused that I defy the keenest critic to say where one begins and the other ends. The homeliest prose melts into the most ethereal poetry – the literal and the imaginative fairly confound their identity.

This, however, is vague praise. Tintoret's great merit, to my mind, was his unequalled distinctness of vision. When once he had conceived the germ of a scene it defined itself to his imagination with an intensity, an amplitude, an individuality of expression, which make one's observation of his pictures seem less an operation of the mind than a kind of supplementary experience of life. Veronese and Titian are content with a much looser specification, as their treatment of any subject that the author of the Crucifixion at San Cassano has also treated abundantly proves. There are few more suggestive contrasts than that between the absence of a total character at all commensurate with its scattered variety and brilliancy in Veronese's *Marriage of Cana*, at the Louvre, and the poignant, almost startling, completeness of Tintoret's illustration of the theme at the Salute church. To compare his *Presentation of the Virgin*, at the Madonna dell' Orto, with Titian's at the Academy, or his *Annunciation* with Titian's close at hand, is to measure the essential difference between observation and imagination. One has certainly not said all that there is to say for Titian when one has called him an observer. *Il y mettait du sien*, and I use the term to designate roughly the artist whose apprehension, infinitely deep and strong when applied to the single figure or to easily balanced groups, spends itself vainly on great dramatic combinations – or rather leaves them ungauged. It was the whole scene that Tintoret seemed to have beheld in a flash of inspiration intense enough to stamp it ineffaceably on his perception; and it was the whole scene, complete, peculiar, individual, unprecedented, that he committed to canvas with all the vehemence of his talent. Compare his *Last Supper*, at San Giorgio – its long, diagonally placed table, its dusky spaciousness, its scattered lamp-light and halo-light, its startled, gesticulating figures, its richly realistic foreground – with the customary formal, almost mathematical rendering of the subject, in which impressiveness seems to have been sought in elimination rather than comprehension. You get from Tintoret's work the impression that he felt, pictorially, the great, beautiful, terrible spectacle of human life very much as Shakespeare felt it poetically – with a heart that never ceased to beat a passionate accompaniment to every stroke of his brush. Thanks to this fact his works are signally grave, and their almost universal and rapidly increasing decay doesn't relieve their gloom. Nothing indeed can well be sadder than the great collection of Tintorets at San Rocco. Incurable blackness is settling fast upon all of them, and they frown at you across the sombre splendour of their great chambers like gaunt twilight phantoms of pictures. To our children's children Tintoret, as things are going, can be hardly more than a name; and such of them as shall miss the tragic beauty, already so dimmed and stained, of the great *Bearing of the Cross* in that temple of his spirit will live and die without knowing the largest eloquence of art. If you wish to add the last touch of solemnity to the place recall as vividly as possible while you linger at San Rocco the painter's singularly interesting portrait of himself, at the Louvre. The old man looks out of the canvas from beneath a brow as sad as a sunless twilight, with just such a stoical hopelessness as you might fancy him to wear if he stood at your side gazing at his rotting canvases. It isn't whimsical to read it as the face of a man who felt that he had given the world more than the world was likely to repay. Indeed before every picture of Tintoret you may remember this tremendous portrait with profit. On one side the power, the passion, the illusion of his art; on the other the mortal fatigue of his spirit. The world's knowledge of him is so small that the portrait throws a doubly precious light on his personality; and when we wonder vainly what manner of man he was, and what were his purpose, his faith and his method, we may find forcible assurance there that they were at any rate his life – one of the most intellectually passionate ever led.

This brief essay (which concludes with some pages about Verona) summarizes the impressions which had been more diffusely expressed in his letters. Written for what his brother William called "newspaporial" circulation, it is focused on a limited selection of topics. And it is still anchored to *The Stones of Venice*. Soon after it was published Charles Eliot Norton wrote to tell James that he had read the passages about Tintoretto to Ruskin: "It would have been pleasant for you to see the cordial admiration he felt for your work and to hear his warm expressions of the good it did him, to find such sympathies and such appreciations, and to know that you were to be added to the little list of those who really and intelligently and earnestly care for the same things that touched him most deeply and influenced his life most powerfully. You may be pleased from your heart to have given not merely pleasure, but stimulus, to a man of genius very solitary, and with few friends who care for what he cares for."[15]

Presumably the reading did not include the lines referring to Ruskin's interpretation of Veronese as "pushing matters too far". But James was soon to cast off almost completely from Ruskin, questioning the central tenet of his philosophy of art. "Art is the one corner of human life in which we may take our ease," he wrote in 1877.[16] "One may read a great many pages of Mr Ruskin without getting a hint of this delightful truth; a hint of the not unimportant fact that art after all is made for us and not we for art. This idea of the value of a work being in the amount of entertainment it yields is conspicuous by its absence. And as for Mr Ruskin's world of art being a place where we may take life easily, woe to the luckless mortal who enters it with any such disposition. Instead of a garden of delight, he finds a sort of assize court, in perpetual session. Instead of a place in which human responsibilities are lightened and suspended he finds a region governed by a kind of Draconic legislation. His responsibilities indeed are tenfold increased; the gulf between truth and error is for ever yawning at his feet; the pains and penalties of this same error are advertised, in apocalyptic terminology, upon a thousand sign-posts; and the rash intruder soon begins to look back with infinite longing to the lost paradise of the artless." The gentle voice of Gautier proclaiming *l'art pour l'art* has prevailed – but only temporarily. For when James later revised the essay for publication in his *Italian Hours*, a significant change was made: "illusion" and not "entertainment" was said to be the value yielded by a work of art.

A Venice in Venice: Whistler

Nine years were to pass before Henry James returned to Venice. In the meantime, both Whistler and Sargent had been there. Whistler had hoped and planned to go to Venice some years earlier, in 1876, but was too deeply absorbed in work on Frederick Leyland's *Peacock Room* (now in the Freer Gallery of Art, Washington, D.C.) in which he over-painted sixteenth-century leather hangings in blue, to harmonize with one of his pictures, and then decorated every available surface with strutting gilded peacocks. Leyland, who suspected his wife of an amorous affair with Whistler, refused to pay either for the work or for the materials and did his damnedest to ruin him financially. A further disaster followed. In November 1878 Whistler was awarded a farthing damages but obliged to pay the heavy costs of his notorious libel suit against Ruskin – the law case which Henry James thought "a singular and most regrettable exhibition". To make ends meet during the legal wranglings Whistler turned to etching which had always been his most reliable source of income. But in May 1879 he was obliged to declare bankruptcy. Two months later friends were said to be helping to pay for him to go to Venice to etch and in September the Fine Art Society of Bond Street – a commercial gallery specializing at this time in graphic work – commissioned from him twelve etchings of Venice and provided a welcome advance of £150.

In mid-September Whistler left London and on the 19th reached Venice, where he was joined by his mistress, Maud Franklin, a month later. He is said to have begun by renting a studio on an upper floor of the magnificent but at this time sadly dilapidated Palazzo Rezzonico on the Grand Canal. A number of artists had studios there –

Whistler, The Bridge, 1879-80

Boldini, for instance, and later Sargent – and it was to be Robert Browning's last home after his son Pen bought it and began restoring it in 1887. Whether or not Whistler worked there, he certainly lived in lodgings on that side of the canal, near the Frari, for the first part of his stay before moving to the far end of the Riva from where several of his finest views were etched or drawn in pastel.

Unlike Henry James, Whistler did not fall in love with Venice at first sight. On New Year's Day 1880 he told his sister that he wished he were in London. "Of course, if things were as they ought to be all would be fit and well and I should be resting happily in the only city in the world fit to live in instead of struggling on in a sort of Opera Comique country when the audience is absent and the season is over."[1] Writing to Marcus Huish, a director of the Fine Art Society, he blamed the Venetian winter for his failure to deliver twelve etchings by 20th December as stipulated in his contract. It was one of the coldest ever recorded. "I can't fight against the gods – with whom I am generally a favorite – and not come to grief – so that now – at this very moment – I am an invalid and a prisoner – because I rashly thought I might hasten matters by standing in the snow with a plate in my hand and an icicle at the end of my nose … here in Venice there has been a steady hardening of every faculty belonging to the painter for the last two months and a half at least – during which time you might as well have proposed to etch on a block of Wenham Lake as to have done anything with a copper plate that involves holding it!"[2] But he went on to claim that his prints "will be superb – and you may double your bets all round… I have learned to know a Venice in Venice that the others seem never to have perceived… The etchings themselves are far more delicate in execution, more beautiful in subject, and more important in interest than any of the old set." Nor was his claim exaggerated.

Whistler, The Balcony, 1879-80

*Whistler, The Steps,
1879-80*

A dedicated *plein-airiste*, Whistler roamed the city with prepared copper plates and an etching needle in the way most artists carry a sketchbook and pencil. By the end of 1879 he had probably etched as many as sixteen plates and before he returned to England he had brought the number up to about fifty. He was intent, in the first place, on recording his visual impressions of this most obviously picturesque – most paintable and most frequently painted – of all cities. Venice presented a challenge to a "modern" artist such as Whistler, whose recent aestheticism overlay, without suppressing, the more deeply felt "realism" of his years in France with Courbet and other avant-garde painters. For them, as for Baudelaire, the "city" was the subject *par excellence* for a painter of "modern life". Whistler had already confronted the problem in London where he had sought out working-class districts, especially the squalid, indeed dangerous and polluted, riverside districts of Wapping and Rotherhithe: and Baudelaire had noticed his Thames etchings approvingly as an instance of a "modern" artist's interpretation of the city. But Venice was a much greater challenge. Wandering down insalubrious alleys and glimpsing from occasional bridges obscure, stagnant canals, he explored areas of the city until then disregarded by artists and transformed them into poetic visions of melancholy, evanescent beauty. He found a "Venice in Venice" all his own. It was a feat of the artistic imagination which he was afterwards to describe in words – was he thinking of Venice or of London, or of both? – when he spoke of how "the evening mist clothes the waterside with poetry, as with a veil, and the poor buildings lose themselves in the dim sky, and the tall chimneys become *campanili*, and the warehouses are palaces in the night, and the whole city hangs in the heavens,"[3] and Nature sings, for once, in tune and sings her exquisite song for the artist alone.

Eventually he was to hire, by the month, a gondolier, Cavaldoro, who "came to know with his Italian intuition just where Whistler most desired to go". The American artist Otto Bacher wrote, "If he did not ride, he would follow his master, carrying the paraphernalia under his arm." Materials were always to hand; prepared etching plates, sheets of variously coloured paper and two boxes of pastels, "an older one for instant use, filled with little bits of strange, broken colors, and a newer box with which he did his principal work."[4] And as he was rowed through the minor canals or walked along the *fondamente* that fringed them, or made his way through dark narrow *calli*, with names evoking the remote history of the Republic, into the sunlit spaces of *campi, campielli* and courtyards with their carved stone well-heads, his attention would be caught by a succession of objects for his needle or crayons – sometimes palatial façades but more often simple houses or workshops, with here a bridge, there the entrance to a neglected garden. He said that one winter evening he had strayed into a courtyard so absolutely beautiful and so perfect a picture that it was impossible for him to draw it.

During his first winter in Venice, Whistler had quickly struck up a friendship with the Californian artist William Graham.[5] Graham was a topographical painter of some talent, as well as being the American vice-consul, and he became Whistler's great friend and stand-by, helping him in numerous practical

Whistler, The Garden, 1879-80

Otto Henry Bacher, Near the Casa Jankovitz, where Whistler lodges, c.1880

ways. But with the arrival of Frank Duveneck[6] and other young American artists in the spring, Whistler found himself being lionized once again and he was to spend a great deal of his time that summer with "the Duveneck boys". Some of them paid him the compliment of imitation and one or two, notably Otto Henry Bacher, recorded their memories of him in Venice. It was as "a curious sailor-like stranger"[7] that he was first spotted by Bacher; "short, thick and wiry, with a head that seemed large and out of proportion to the lithe figure. His large, wide-brimmed, soft, brown hat was tilted far back, and suggested a brown halo. It was a background for his curly black hair and singular white lock, high over his right eye, like a fluffy feather carelessly left where it had lodged. A dark sack coat almost covered an extremely low turned-down collar, while a narrow black ribbon did service as a tie, the long pennant-like ends of which, flapping about, now and then hit his single eye-glass." Bacher was a member of a small travelling art school which spent its winters in Florence and summers in Venice under the direction of Frank Duveneck, a rough thread in the intricate web of American expatriate society. In 1880 Duveneck was courting and later married Lizzie Boott whose father, long resident in Florence, was an old family friend of Henry James. (Lizzie was the "original" of Pansy in *The Portrait of a Lady*.)

Duveneck hailed from Kentucky and had studied in Munich together with two other Americans, William Merritt Chase and John Henry Twachtman, who also painted in Venice. In 1878, having made some reputation for himself, he began his long career as a teacher of American artists. James called him "a child of nature and a child of freedom", a "very good fellow" despite his "roughness, want of education, of a language, etc." and was rather impressed by his "remarkably strong and brilliant work", though it

Naya studio, Castello quarter, c.1880

Robert Frederick Blum, No doubt this is "Jimmy", Venice 1880

followed a distinctly Germanic brand of realism. Lizzie Boott remarked that "the very genius of ugliness seems to possess him". He was an unlikely friend for the aesthetic Francophile butterfly, Whistler. Nevertheless, Whistler moved from the centre of the city, where he and Maud had spent the winter, to a lodging in the Casa Jankovitz at the end (the unfashionable end Lady Bracknell would have called it) of the Riva degli Schiavoni on the corner of the present day via Garibaldi, in order to have the company of Duveneck and his pupils – perhaps also to benefit from a breezier situation and better views which he both etched and drew in pastel from the windows of his room. Here, a far cry from the exquisitely decorated and furnished White House in Chelsea which he had had to sell to pay his debts, he returned to the *vie bohème* of his student days in Paris, though he was now regarded as very much the "master" by Duveneck's "boys", as the students were called. He commanded their services and they helped him to pull proofs of his etchings and assisted in other ways. "Whistler, I hear, has been borrowing money from everybody, and from some who can ill afford to spare it," a disenchanted English artist, Henry Woods, reported in the autumn of 1880.[8] "He shared a studio for five or six months with a young fellow called Jobbins. Jobbins could never work there with him in it. He (Whistler) invited people there as to his own place, and has never paid a penny rent. He used all the colours he could lay his hands upon; he uses a large flat brush which he calls 'Matthew', and this brush is the terror of about a dozen young Americans he is with now. Matthew takes up a whole tube of cobalt at a lick; of course the colour is somebody else's property. There are all sorts of conspiracies against Whistler. He is an epidemic, and old-man-of-the-sea. These young chaps were quite flattered at first when he joined them. It made me roar when I heard of his goings on among them, he evidently pays for nothing. There is no mistake that he is the cheekiest scoundrel out – a regular Ally Sloper. I am giving him a wide berth. It's really awful. There will be *Grande Festa* if he ever goes away." This seems, however, to have been a minority opinion. Whistler was generally accepted, indeed welcomed, as a "character" whose conversation was a rich subject for mimicry, whose pettish humours could be light-heartedly indulged, and whose scrounging could be supported. One of Duveneck's "boys", Charles Abel Corwin, portrayed him in a monotype which suggests the sensitive, deeply serious and even melancholy character beneath the outwardly jaunty persona which Ralph

Charles Abel Corwin, Whistler, 1880

Cherubino Kirchmayr,
Mrs Bronson, 1881

Curtis and others loved to caricature.

Ralph Curtis was another young American artist in Venice but one from a very different social milieu from that of the Duveneck "boys". He was the son of Daniel Curtis who, embittered by an unfortunate incident in his native Boston – he had been provoked into a light assault on a judge who had taken his seat in a railway carriage and was briefly imprisoned as a result – had moved with his wife (the daughter of an English admiral) to Europe where, after some years searching for a suitable residence, he rented and then bought, in 1885, the magnificent Palazzo Barbaro on the Grand Canal in Venice. The undisputed leader of expatriate American society in Venice was, however, Katherine De Kay Bronson in whose salon Whistler was cordially received. Mrs Bronson was a distant relation of his first patron, Thomas De Kay Winans. With her rarely-seen husband Arthur Bronson and their daughter Edith, she had settled in 1876 in Ca' Alvisi, a small palace (by Venetian standards) at the mouth of the Grand Canal directly opposite Santa Maria della Salute. "During many happy years, from lunch till long past bed-time her house was the open rendezvous for the rich and poor – the famous and the famished – *les rois en exil* and the heirs presumptive to the thrones of fame," as Ralph Curtis wrote. "Whistler there had his seat from the first, but to the delight of all he generally held the floor. One night, a curious contrast was the great and genial Robert Browning commenting on the form of a famous 'Jimmy letter' to the *World*."[9]

But sympathetic though he found Ca' Alvisi, it was the company of young artists that Whistler preferred. "Very late, on hot *sirocco* nights, long after the concert crowd had dispersed, one little knot of men might often be seen in the deserted Piazza San Marco, supping refreshment in

Sargent, Edith Bronson,
c.1881

Ralph Curtis, A Nocturne at Mrs Bronson's, 1880

front of Florian's. You might be sure that was Whistler, in white duck, praising France, abusing England, and thoroughly enjoying Italy," to quote Ralph Curtis again. "He was telling how he had seen painting in Paris revolutionized by innovators of 'powerful handling': Manet, Courbet, Vollon, Regnault, Carolus-Duran. He felt more enthusiasm for the then recently resuscitated popularity of Velasquez and Hals." And his young American audience would be dazzled by his conversation and, since most of them were painters too, by his work as well. There was an occasion when a Russian amateur artist with the resounding name of Alexander Nikoljewitsch Wolkoff-Muromzoff (otherwise known as Russoff) claimed that his pastels of Venice were indistinguishable from those by Whistler but he was laughed out of court. For his admirers, Whistler staged a highly characteristic performance, described by Ralph Curtis: "Shortly before his return to England with portfolios of the famous etchings and delicious pastels, he gave his friends a tea-dinner. As seeing the best of his Venetian work was the real feast, the hour for the *hors-d'oeuvres*, consisting of sardines, hard-boiled eggs, fruit, cigarettes, and excellent coffee prepared by the ever-admirable Maud, was arranged for six o'clock. Effective pauses succeeded the presentation of each masterpiece, for with Japanese precision they had to be most carefully fixed in the one mount available. During these *entractes*, Whistler amused his guests with witty conjectures as to the verdict of the grave critics in London on 'these things'. One of his favourite types for sarcasm used to be the eminently respectable Londoner, who is *'always* called at 8.30, close-shaved at quarter to 9, and in the City by 10. What will he make of *this*? Serve him right, too. Ha Ha!'"

The impact made by his Venetian work was immediate. In emulation Frank Duveneck took up etching and some of his prints, when shown in London, were mistakenly supposed to be by Whistler (who was enraged). Similarly his friend Twachtman abandoned the Germanic realist tradition in which he had been trained for the small-scale delicacy of pastels, beginning with misty views of Venetian back-canals.[10] Whistler's "Venice in Venice" soon became the common property of visiting artists and it may be more than a coincidence that Renoir was to make his only visit to Venice shortly after seeing Whistler

Ralph Curtis, Whistler, 1880

in Paris in the spring of 1881. For he had created a unique vision of the most frequently painted city in the world.

Whistler, The Riva, 1879-80

Frank Duveneck, The Riva, 1880

"Venice is an impossible place to sit down and sketch in," Whistler told Edith Bronson. He always felt "there was something still better round the corner".[11] And his etchings and pastels convey precisely this impression of views glimpsed before moving on, rather than of something closely studied and fixed (though in fact each one was the product of several sessions *sur le motif*). They made a notable advance on his earlier etched work – especially his almost panoramic, wide-angled views of the Thames – in their development of an extremely loose and free type of composition which dispensed altogether with general outlines in order to work outwards from a single, carefully chosen feature to less sharply perceived surrounding motifs and on to an often completely dissolving and indistinct periphery. "I began first of all by seizing upon the chief point of interest," he remarked.[12] "Perhaps it might have been the extreme distance – the little palaces and the shipping beneath the bridge. If so I would begin drawing that distance in elaborately and then would expand from it until I came to the bridge, which I would draw in one broad sweep. If by chance I did not see the whole of the bridge, I would not put it in. In this way the picture must necessarily be a perfect thing from start to finish." His etchings were, in fact, conceived as *objets d'art*, as precious as the pieces of Japanese porcelain he so loved, to be visually grasped as a whole and then examined in detail rather than "read" from left to right, foreground to background. (The scenes are shown in reverse, in fact, but this did not trouble Whistler though some of his admirers, such as Sickert,[13] wanted them reversed back in photographic reproductions.) This is very obviously true of the great *Upright Venice* in which a large space – a kind of eloquent silence – is left blank in the centre, demanding mute contemplation like a Japanese *kakemono*. And again and again these extraordinary etchings recapture

Whistler, A Venetian Canal, 1879-80

Whistler, Upright Venice,
1879-80

the sensations of a stroller whose eye is suddenly delighted by some strange or beautiful and always unexpected surprise, from the bend of every canal and the top of every bridge.

Venice is predominently a city of façades: only the largest buildings are sufficiently detached to be seen three-dimensionally. Indeed, it often has the appearance of a series of theatrical back-cloths; but the drama of life is played out behind rather than in front of them. Whistler indicates this secret, private world with the utmost tact. In more than one plate he focused on a mysteriously dark open doorway with a penumbra of weathered architectural decoration. On this threshold of the unknown a dyer rinses a swathe of cloth in the canal, a ghost-like girl waits while a boatman pauses in his *sandolo*. But generally

Whistler, The Beggars, 1879-80

there are few figures visible – except in the Piazzetta, along the Riva or on the steep slopes of the Rialto Bridge. Seated women sometimes string beads in a courtyard; listless beggars hold out their hands for alms in a *sottoportico*; gondoliers row their craft with their peculiar methodical slowness on the lagoon or sit waiting by a landing-stage. In several plates there is no sign of life at all. And the series as a whole insidiously conveys the silence and stillness of Venice, broken now and then by a cry echoing through the labyrinth of winding canals, a silence noted by travellers from other cities where the rattle of iron wheels and the clatter of horses on cobbled streets was continuous – as well as the lethargy induced by the *sirocco*, that enervating south wind that drifts up the Adriatic.

Not that Whistler himself succumbed to the prevailing indolence. His months in Venice were among the most productive of his life – so much so that he was to be intermittently occupied in preparing his etched plates for publication until the 1890s, adding, subtracting, substituting details for up to fifteen different "states" as the different printings or editions of an etching are called. He also painted in oils some seven or eight views, accounts of which are rather vague. Only two can now be traced, both nocturnes in which conventional subjects are shown in a new Whistlerian light – or rather dimness. One, *Nocturne: Blue and Gold* is of the Piazza San Marco late at night with a few gas jets flickering and the great Basilica an insubstantial presence – off-centre and with the south bay cut off. It would no doubt have seemed sacrilegious to Ruskin, for the sculptural decoration he extolled is barely visible; indeed the scene is rendered in much the same manner as the *Nocturne in Black and Gold* of London, which Ruskin had deplored as "flinging a pot of paint in the public's face" – the remark that led to the notorious libel action, Whistler's bankruptcy and, ironically, to his fourteen months in Venice. The other surviving Venetian painting is a twilight rather than a truly nocturnal view of San Giorgio Maggiore, with gleams of light in the monastic buildings and on the low line of the distant Lido. Ghostly gondolas glide stealthily across the foreground. These oils, unlike the etchings and pastels, were painted from memory. Bacher recorded how night after night Whistler "watched the gondolas pass, singly and in groups with lanterns waving in the darkness, without making a stroke with brush or pen. Then he would return to his rooms and paint the scene, or as much as he could remember, going again and again to refresh some particular impression."[14] But painting was for him a minor, almost spare-time, activity in Venice. When he was not etching he was working in pastel, a medium he began to exploit at this time with an entirely new awareness of its possibilities.

"This evening the weather softened slightly and perhaps tomorrow may be fine – and then Venice will be simply glorious as now and then I have seen it," he wrote to his mother.[15] "After the wet, the colors upon the walls and their reflections in the canals are more gorgeous than ever – and with the sun shining upon the polished marble mingled with rich toned bricks and plaster, this amazing city of palaces becomes really a fairyland – created, one would think, especially for the painter. The people with their gay gowns and handkerchiefs – and the many tinted buildings for them to lounge against or pose before, seem to exist especially for one's pictures – and to have no other reason for being! One could certainly spend years here and never lose the freshness that pervades the place." Such effects he caught in his pastels, about a hundred all told. Otto Bacher saw him at work and described his technique: "He had quantities of vari-colored papers, browns, reds, grays uniform in

Whistler, The Lagoon, Venice: Nocturne in Blue and Silver, 1879-80

Whistler, San Giovanni Evangelista, 1879-80

size. In beginning a pastel he drew his subject crisply and carefully in outline with black crayon upon one of these sheets of tinted paper which fitted the general color of the motive. A few touches with sky-tinted pastels, corresponding to nature, produced a remarkable effect, with touches of reds, grays, and yellows for the buildings here and there. Some motives were finished at one sitting, but more often he made only the crayon outline … leaving the unfinished sketch for days … to be filled in later with pastels."[16] Tell-tale pin-holes show how often some sheets were re-attached to the drawing board for further work, revealing that their appearance of spontaneity was (as is nearly always the case) achieved by careful deliberation.

In his pastels he concentrated, of course, on catching effects of light and colour outside the range of monochrome etchings. One of the finest is a distant view of the Salute and the entrance to the Grand Canal at a moment when the sky, the sea and the buildings all shimmer and melt together in the soft, powdery light – for which pastels were the ideal medium. A few are of subjects so pictorially irresistible that they had often been depicted before, though never with such concentration and atmospheric finesse – occasionally, very occasionally, of buildings of some architectural distinction such as the Scuola di San Giovanni Evangelista, a masterpiece of Venetian early renaissance architecture – also very occasionally remote parts of the city which no longer survive, having been completely built over since Whistler's day, such as the Santa Marta area beyond the present day Piazzale Roma. But many more are, like the etchings, of previously unregarded fragments of the urban fabric – narrow *calli* penetrated by light at either end only, sequestered courtyards where women draw water from wells and, exceptionally, an interior of some formerly grandiose patrician residence now reduced to indigence, to a "Palace in Rags".[17] No other artist – not even Canaletto – more fully exploited the pictorial possibilities of a city which is so much more than a display of architectural masterpieces and which, to the present day, is the only one in the world where it is possible to wander for a couple of hours without being confronted with a single eyesore.

"I wish I could show you some of the lovely pastels I have done. I told you I should discover something new," Whistler wrote to his friend Charles Augustus Howell on 26th January 1880.[18] "The work I do is lovely, and these other fellows here have no idea! no distant idea! of what I see with certainty." It was easier for him to work in pastel than to draw with an etching needle out

Whistler, The Giudecca, 1879-80

FEBRUARY 12, 1881.]   PUNCH,

WHISTLER'S WENICE; OR, PASTELS BY PASTELTHWAITE.

MR. WHISTLER is the artful Doger of Venice. TURNER made "studies" from which he subsequently developed his pictures: but Mr. WHISTLER is the "Chiel amang ye taking notes"—in colour, and, unable to keep them to himself, he exhibits them in the most generous and self-effacing way to the public generally. It is very kind of him; perhaps it is very deep of him. Does he want to discourage his brother artists from going to Venice? He may have conceived a violent animosity to Mr. COOK, and has hit upon this method of deterring intending tourists from visiting the "Pride of the Sea."

Whatever the motive for the exhibition, the artist seems to speak for himself, and say—"Well, Sir, I'm Master JIMMY WHISTLER I am, and if I can do this sort o' thing with a shilling box o' paints from the Lowther Arcade, a few sheets of blotting paper, and some brown-paper covers off the family jam-pots, I could do bigger work with improved materials, you bet!"

This address evidently conveys the suggestion that he should be forthwith presented by his friends and admirers with a real colour-box and the entire artistic paraphernalia. In furtherance of this design, we place before our readers our own "Notes" in black and white, suggested by those of Master WHISTLER.

N.B.—Visitors are requested to observe the principal figures, on which we only allow ourselves to touch lightly, and compare them with those in the brown-paper Catalogue. These notes being intended for practical guidance, every visitor should take them to the Gallery as a suggestive commentary which will be of the greatest assistance to him in appreciating the collection in detail.

No. 1. *Sotto Portico, San Giacomo.* A sort o' portico. Pretty clear so far.

No. 7. *The Little Back Canal.* Subject from the celebrated Triumviretta, *Coxio e Boxio.*

Sergento Bouncero. Don't be angry, Gentlemen. There used to be a Little Back Canal here.

Boxio e Coxio (together). Then put it up!   [*Exit* BOUNCERO.

No. 10.

No. 10. *Nocturne—The Riva.* A Mud-bank note. "First Impression of Venice on a piece of Blotting-Paper."

No. 13. *The Giudecca: note in flesh-colour.* Suggestion for a Picture to represent Mr. IRVING as *Shylock* on a river—somewhere. Note for Jewdecca-rative Art.

No. 14. *The Bridge—flesh-colour and brown.* Suggestion for Sir WILLIAM TITE's pantaloons—say a pair of Tite's.

No. 18. *Nocturne at a Hotel.* Curious specimens of shoes left outside the bedroom doors to be cleaned. Suggestion for the Boots.

No. 21. *Fish Market, San Barnabo.* Suggestion of trade being very dull.

No. 22. *The Old Marble Palace.* We "dreamt that we dwelt in marble halls," and awoke with a severe cold. About this period we came to the conclusion, that if we wisited Wenice —WHISTLER's Wenice—we should soon become what Mr. MANTALINI described as a "demm'd moist uncomfortable body."

No. 18.

No. 27. *Campanile at Lido.* Suggestion for a camp in ile—this isn't in ile. *Note*—it's out in the desolate country, a truly-rural-Lido sort of place.

No. 28. "*Boat Ahoy!*" Suggestion for a picture of "there were three sailors of Bristol City, Who took a boat and went to sea."

No. 29. *The Giudecca—Winter: grey and blue.* Uncomfortably suggestive of a nervous man bent on taking a header.

No. 35. *The Staircase: note in red.* Suggestion that this note "should be taken as red."

No. 36. *The Cemetery.* This is what Master JAMES calls it. We prefer to consider it as suggestion for a dark scene in some

No. 29.

Pantomime of *Gulliver*, representing *Gulliver's* cocked-hat adrift off Lilliput or Water-Lilliput.

No. 37. *Swamped Buttercups.*

No. 38. *The Red Doorway.* Suggestion for the Home of SMUDGE, R.A.

No. 39. Suggestion for a view of the Polar Regions "from the steps of the Piazetta."

No. 43. *A Red Note.* Suggestive that bearer waits answer.

No. 47. *Awfully Cowl'd!* Suggestion for a picture representing three unfortunate Pierrots who, returning from a fancy ball in the country, have lost their way and stuck in a peat-bog.

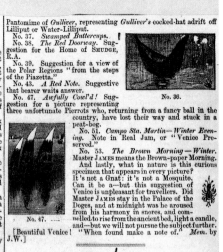

No. 36.

No. 51. *Campo Sta. Martin—Winter Evening.* Note in Real Jam, or "Venice Preserved."

No. 53. *The Brown Morning—Winter.* Master JAMES means the Brown-paper Morning.

And lastly, what in nature is this curious specimen that appears in every picture? It's not a Gnat: it's not a Mosquito. Can it be a—but this suggestion of Venice is unpleasant for travellers. Did Master JAMES stay in the Palace of the Doges, and at midnight was he aroused from his harmony in snores, and compelled to rise from the ancient bed, light a candle, and—but we will not pursue the subject further.

No. 47.

[Beautiful Venice! "When found make a note of." *Mem.* by J.W.]

IO TRIUMPHE!

of doors in the icy weather, even on sunny days which are not infrequent in the Venetian winter when the whole city is suddenly illuminated, as it were, in relief – the *calli* seem darker, the open spaces brighter and the clear, sharp light picks out details of decoration on the buildings. Sunsets are never more brilliantly flamboyant than at this time of year, as several of Whistler's pastels record. But he continued with his pastels in the soft caressing light of summer. And in the autumn he referred to those he had completed in the course of a year as "absolute beauties", claiming that "painter fellows here, who have seen them, are quite startled at their brilliancy".[19]

Eventually, towards the end of November, he dragged himself away from Venice very reluctantly, hoping to return one day though he was never able to do so. Immediately after he arrived in London he exhibited twelve of his Venetian etchings at the Fine Arts Society in Bond Street where he made a second *entré* into the artistic world of the capital, stepping lightly out of a hansom cab with his long cane in one hand, leading by a ribbon a beautiful little white Pomeranian dog. The exhibition aroused enough interest to be reported with some praise and rather more abuse in the press. A few sets of the etchings were sold. At the end of the following January he staged an exhibition of fifty-three pastels in a room decorated according to his instructions and described by his friend, the architect E.W. Godwin ("the greatest aesthete of them all" according to Oscar Wilde): "First a low skirting of yellow gold, then a high dado of dull yellow green cloth, then a moulding of green gold, and then a frieze and ceiling of pale reddish brown. The frames are arranged 'on the line', but here and there one is placed over another. Most of the frames and mounts are of rich yellow gold, but a dozen out of the fifty-three are of green gold, dotted about with a view to decoration, and eminently successful in attaining it."[20] According to Maud Franklin "all the London world was at the private view – princesses, painters, beauties, actors – everybody – in fact at one moment of the day it was impossible to move – for the room was crammed." And the press was generally favourable though *Punch* did not forgo the opportunity to mock. Godwin called many of the exhibits masterpieces, praising one "where the old stained plaster of the wall looks as if we could peel it off in slabs if we could but get a trowel behind it" suggesting "a detachment from the actual wall that will some day bring about its fall and ruin". A view at the junction of two canals was "extremely simple, full of

Whistler, Nocturne: San Giorgio, 1879-80

repose, and wonderfully suggestive of the noiselessness of the place." Another critic remarked that "Venice floating among her opal skies, or wrapped in her robes of blue and grey, is impressed on our memory by these pastels."

Henry James was in London at the time and must have heard about these exhibitions even if he did not go to them. He had met Whistler in 1878, a "queer but entertaining creature" whom he thought a "little Londonized Southerner who paints abominably"[21] though his etchings were "altogether admirable".[22] The views of Venice may perhaps have spurred him to return there for an extended stay in the spring of 1881. Later he was to know Whistler better (though he was never to be on such friendly terms with him as he was with Sargent) and also to appreciate his paintings. And many years later, after Whistler's death, James was to give full approval to the illustrations drawn in pastel in his style by his closest follower, Joseph Pennell, for the Venetian and other essays in *Italian Hours*.

Par temps gris: Sargent

John Singer Sargent, twenty-two years younger than Whistler, was a distant cousin and close friend and fellow student in Paris of Ralph Curtis who nicknamed him "Scamps" and probably introduced him to Whistler in Venice. His father, Fitzwilliam Sargent – formerly a doctor of medicine in Philadelphia and author of a textbook on surgery – was a reluctant, and his mother a

determined, American expatriate: from 1854 onwards they had wandered round Europe, stopping in the winters where it was relatively warm and the summers where it was fairly cool. They were in Florence in January 1856 when their son was born, and he grew up virtually unschooled but highly educated, fluent in French, German and Italian as well as precociously talented in art and music. Not until he was twenty did he go to America, and then only briefly; nor was he ever to stay there for more than short visits, though he always regarded himself as an American. Whistler spent rather more time in the United States, but he had left, never to return, in 1855

when he was twenty-one. Both were trained in Paris before settling in London, and neither fitted squarely into the American, French or British school of painting.

In 1874 Sargent began to study in Paris under Charles-Emile-Auguste Duran, who had adopted Carolus-Duran as his *nom de brosse*, one of the most successful portrait painters of the time, the master of a style which departed just far enough from the academic norm to please fashionable society. The master-pupil relationship was a singularly happy one and Sargent scored his first public success in the Salon of 1879 with a portrait of Carolus-Duran which demonstrated how much he had learned. He also came to share Carolus-Duran's admiration for Velázquez and Hals, some of whose works he copied. It was to study Hals that he went to the Netherlands in the spring of 1880 with Ralph Curtis whose portrait he sketched on the beach at Scheveningen. This was a *mouvementé* year for Sargent. In January he had been in Algeria and

Tunisia; in September he joined his parents at Aix-les-Bains and from there went with them to Venice, putting up at the Hotel d'Italie, on the site of the present Hotel Bauer Grünwald on the Grand Canal.

He may have gone to Venice partly, if not mainly, just to be with his parents who had characteristically chosen to be there for the month reputedly the best for the weather, neither too hot nor too chilly. But he soon settled down to painting and on 22nd September his sister wrote: "He expects to remain on here indefinitely, as long as he finds he can work with advantage, and has taken a studio in the Palazzo Rezzonico, Canal Grande, an immense house where several artists are installed and where one of his Paris friends has also taken a room to work in."[1] On the 27th he wrote to refuse an invitation to stay with friends in Florence, Mrs Paget and her family whom he had known since childhood – Violet Paget had just begun to make a name for herself as "Vernon Lee", writing with great perception and originality on eighteenth-century Italian literature and music. "Much as I would like to see you and your son again and renew my old *bonne camaraderie* with Violet," he wrote, "I am forced to consider that there may be only a few more weeks of pleasant season here and I must make the most of them… I must do something for the Salon and have determined to stay as late as possible in Venice."[2] When his parents left he moved from the Hotel d'Italie to lodgings in Piazza San Marco, next to the clock-tower, but continued to work in his studio in Palazzo Rezzonico, and stayed on well into the next year, perhaps as late as March. In 1882 he was in Venice again, staying from August until late November with the Curtises in the part of Palazzo Barbaro they were then renting. Probably in gratitude for this hospitality he painted a portrait of Mrs Curtis – a more tender and intimate work than his likenesses of fashionable Parisian sitters.

During these two early visits to Venice Sargent painted more than

Sargent, Mrs Curtis, 1882

*Sargent,
Ramón Subercaseaux,
1880*

twenty canvases and also many watercolours, few of which can be precisely dated. However, a brilliant, freely painted study of a man in a gondola must have been done shortly after his arrival for it represents a friend from Paris (mentioned by his sister in her letter of 22nd September) who had also taken a studio in Palazzo Rezzonico: Ramón Subercaseaux. He was a Chilean diplomat and amateur painter of whose wife Sargent painted a formal portrait the following year which won a medal at the 1881 Salon. His sparkling, splashy Venetian sketch of Subercaseaux contrasts very strikingly, however, with most of his Venetian paintings, especially with *Venise par temps gris* which was

Sargent, Venise par temps gris, 1880-81

57

Renoir, Fog in Venice, 1881

painted only slightly later, during the autumn or winter of 1880-81. This remarkable painting, the finest of all Sargent's views of Venice, perfectly catches the sad, empty, lost, "out-of-season" atmosphere of the city at this time of year: the lagoon is still, a veil of mist hangs over the buildings in the windless air and all colours are reduced to subtle nuances. Shortly after returning to Paris in 1882 he recalled the previous winter in a letter to Mrs Curtis: "If you stay there late enough you will perhaps see how curious Venice looks with some snow clinging to the roofs and balconies, with a dull sky and the canals of a dull opaque green, not unlike pea soup, *con rispetto*, and very different from the *julienne* of the Grand Canal in summer."[3]

More than any of his other works, *Venise par temps gris* owes a debt to Whistler whose etchings and pastels of Venice Sargent had perhaps seen in the early autumn of 1880. Its poetic haziness and careful though apparently casual disposition of figures, seen at a distance and from a considerable height, suggest that it was painted from or near to one of Whistler's favourite points of vantage, perhaps even from Whistler's window at Casa Jankovitz. But it was also a kind of riposte to Whistler's nocturnes of Venice – a more naturalistic reply to their poetical, elegiac interpretation of the scene. And if Renoir saw it when he was in Venice in the autumn of 1881, it may well have been this Sargent painting rather than anything Whistler had shown him or told him[4] that prompted his *Fog in Venice*. This was not only painted from the same viewpoint as the Sargent but, in its muted, opalescent colours and melancholy, semi-deserted atmosphere, is quite unlike Renoir's other Venetian paintings. They are all of well-known, not to say hackneyed, subjects and sights in vibrant, sparkling sunshine. (He was aware of this himself, writing to friends from Venice that he had "made a study of the Doges' Palace, as if that had never been done before … six painters were queued up to paint it!"[5])

Sargent had discovered his own "Venice in Venice", different from that of Whistler though both artists sought out the remoter and poorer quarters of the city, little or not at all known to foreigners and previously neglected by painters. Moreover, having no commission from a dealer for a set of Venetian views, Sargent was able to depart still further than had Whistler from the conventional. The great and famous Venetian buildings didn't interest him (though they did some years later): he had an eye only for what we would now call vernacular architecture – the simple, traditionally designed buildings

Sargent, Ponte Panada:
Fondamenta Nuove, 1880

on the Merceria, for example, by the beauty and value of which his friend Vernon Lee had also just then been struck. "There," she wrote, "in those tall dark houses, with their dingy look-out on to narrow canals floating wisps of straw, or on to dreary little treeless, grassless squares, in those houses is the real wealth, the real honour, the real good of Venice: there, and not in the palaces of the Grand Canal."[6] On the Fondamenta Nuove, for instance, the bleak north-eastern limits of the city facing a lonely expanse of lagoon, Sargent found the subject of one of his finest watercolours: a simple bridge over the Rio della Panada, a gondola idling in the foreground and simple houses with tall, typically Venetian chimney-stacks beyond. One of his early watercolours is of a small canal junction with the dank lower storeys of minor palaces, a round headed portal and two medieval windows only summarily indicated. It is a twilight scene with the flicker of a gas lamp brightening in the gathering dusk. So too is a still more unusual glimpse of a *calle* flanked by plain workaday buildings – one of those into which lost pedestrians stray in the hope of finding a way out. Another *calle*, where the upper floor of a house has been corbelled out to gain a few extra inches of precious living space, is the subject of a painting in oils, powerful in its sense of gloom and even of menace, redolent of the foetid, unhealthy slums in which cholera was often rampant.

These eerily deserted scenes which so effectively evoke the silence of the under-populated city are unusual, not only in the work of Sargent. When he set up his easel in less remote and insalubrious quarters he focused attention on the daily life of

Sargent, Venice, 1880-81

Sargent, A Venetian Street, 1882

ordinary people in their extraordinary environment, for it was this combination of the commonplace and the unique, of today and yesterday, that gave Venice its peculiar allure. Figures had seldom been more than incidental in Whistler's Venetian scenes, and proofs of his etchings reveal that he sometimes inserted, removed or replaced them in drypoint after he had drawn the architectural subject. For Sargent, on the other hand, they were often the point of departure. This is very striking in one of the very few of his early watercolours to include well-known buildings, the *Café on the Riva degli Schiavoni* in which the church of the Salute, Sansovino's great library and the Doges' Palace in sharp foreshortening are simply the background for a wintry café scene. (The café was the once famous Orientale now replaced by the annexe to the Hotel Danieli.) In a watercolour of the Campo dei Frari (see p. 102) only a part of the north transept of the great church is visible, to the right of a group of plain buildings behind the two prominent figures in the foreground. In another

Sargent, Campo behind the Scuola di San Rocco, 1880-82

painting of the same year, *Sortie de l'Eglise*, now known only from Sargent's drawing after it, the church is so summarily indicated that it cannot be identified. It was the women walking away from it that interested Sargent. Most striking of all is his painting of the *campo* behind – not in front of – the magnificent Scuola di San Rocco, where, once again, the focus is on the women, with shawls over their heads, in the foreground. They are cut off by the frame, an impressionist's device to lend a casual, arbitrary appearance to the subject – just a fleeting moment caught instantaneously as in a snapshot. This painting especially, in its extraordinary naturalism, contrasts with his other, slightly later, Venetian figurative scenes painted from rather obviously "posed" models.

Venetian life fascinated many late nineteenth-century artists and the Paris Salon and official Academies all over Europe regularly exhibited Venetian genre scenes alongside those of Spanish gypsy and Moroccan and other *orientaliste* subjects. Sargent's painting trips to Spain and North Africa before he went to Venice in 1880 were certainly made with this in mind as, probably, was his visit to Venice as well. When he told Mrs Paget that autumn that "I must do something for the Salon" he was evidently thinking of working up in the studio some of his *sur le motif* sketches into compositions suitable for public exhibition. It was in this way, surely, that he created *Venetian Water Carriers* (see p.73). In some obscure courtyard, where the pavement was uneven and plaster flaked off the walls, two women are filling buckets from an unpretentious *vera di pozzo* or well-head – not one of the many which were richly carved and starred in the guide-

Sargent, A Street in Venice, 1882

Sargent, Café on the Riva degli Schiavoni, c.1881

Sargent, A Venetian Interior, 1880-81

books. Though depicted from life the figures seem to have been posed, rather carefully posed indeed – quite unlike those in *Campo behind the Scuola di San Rocco*. Even more obviously "posed" and studio based are other street scenes of these years in which one or two cloaked figures were inserted into paintings of dank *calli*, palely loitering in the half-light. They serve only to introduce an unhappy and distinctly *voulu* sense of mystery, not without a hint of Grand Guignol. Ralph Curtis suggested *Flirtation Lugubre* as a title for one of them.

Sargent's Venetian interiors were no doubt evolved in much the same way but they are more successful because closer to what he had observed and sometimes painted from life. A watercolour of a frail old woman making lace or crochetwork and another woman stringing beads with her friend in the background, set in the large empty ground-floor hall of some abandoned *palazzo*, is the origin or one of the origins of this series of paintings. The upstairs hall or *portego* rather than a downstairs hall is usually their setting. The *portego* was roofed with dark cross-beams and the light admitted from windows at either end is reflected upwards by the smooth *terrazzo* (marble-paste) floor, icy-cold in winter and cool even at the height of summer. In such rooms – one from that in Palazzo Rezzonico, others perhaps from an upper floor of Palazzo Barbaro before it was bought and restored by the Curtises in 1885 – Sargent posed his Venetian models, idling, gossiping, sorting onions or lethargically stringing beads. Bead stringing was, of course, a characteristic feature of Venetian life and both Whistler and Sargent painted it. One of Sargent's best Venetian paintings is of a glass factory where the beads were made by drawing out rods of the molten material and cutting them into small pieces.

Martin Brimmer, a trustee of the Boston Museum of Fine Arts, noticed some of these pictures when he was in Palazzo Barbaro one day in 1882 and thought them "very clever but a good deal inspired by the desire of finding what no one else has sought here – unpicturesque subjects, absence of colour, absence of sunlight. It seems hardly worthwhile to travel so far for these."[7] Much the same reaction was expressed by Arthur Baignères in the *Gazette des Beaux Arts* when Sargent showed some of his Venetian paintings at the first exhibition of the Société Internationale des Peintres et Sculpteurs in Paris the following year. "We will see neither the Grand Canal nor the Piazza San Marco in these paintings; all that is banal and old-hat. Mr Sargent leads us into out-of-the-way back-alleys and into low ceilinged rooms whose pitch darkness is cut through only by a ray of sunlight. Where have the beautiful women painted by Titian concealed themselves? For it is certainly not their descendants whom we can barely make out beneath their unkempt hair and old black shawls which they wrap round themselves as if shivering with fever. What is the point of going to Italy to record impressions of this kind?"[8] These comments recall those made about the Impressionists who had sought subjects of "modern life" in the Paris outskirts, in the city's *banlieue*. Of course, Sargent knew such Impressionist paintings – he was on friendly terms with

Sargent, Venetian Women in Palazzo Rezzonico, c.1880

Sargent, Venetian Glass Workers, 1880-82

several of the Impressionists and was even invited to exhibit with them in Paris – but it would be specious to draw any parallel between them.

The merits of Sargent's Venetian paintings were recognized, however, by Henry James. He recalled one (or more probably two which he conflated in his mind) among those exhibited in London in 1882 at the Grosvenor Gallery, that conventicle of the aesthetes. It was "a pure gem," he wrote, "representing a small group of Venetian girls of the lower class, sitting in gossip together one summer's day in the big, dim hall of a shabby old *palazzo*. The shutters let in a chink of light: the *scagliola* pavement gleams faintly in it: the whole place is bathed in a kind of transparent shade; the tone of the picture is dark and cool. The girls are vaguely engaged in some very humble household work; they are counting turnips or stringing onions, and these small vegetables, enchantingly painted, look as valuable as pearls."[9]

Delighted Senses and Divided Mind

In February 1881 James had nearly finished writing *The Portrait of a Lady* which was being published serially in the *Atlantic Monthly*. "I wished to get away from the London crowd, the London hubbub, all the entanglements and interruptions of London life; and to quietly bring my novel to a close. So I planned to betake myself to Venice," he recalled a few months later.[1] He arrived on 25th March and instead of staying at a hotel took rooms on the Riva where he lodged until the end of June (apart from an excursion to Rome and a few days on the Venetian mainland). No longer a tourist picking his way from one Ruskin-indexed masterpiece to another, he began to see the city with the eyes of an *habitué*.

During the nine years that had passed since his former visits he had changed: the spruce, bearded, somewhat Frenchified figure who arrived in 1881 was a successful novelist permanently resident in London where he had become a social lion. But Venice was also changing. On his last visit, in 1872, he had already noticed that the Lido was being "sadly 'improved'". The formerly deserted beaches and dunes were being transformed into a "site of delights" with a bathing establishment and an "immense salon" where an orchestra of men in dress coats played "a pot-pourri from *Faust*" – so the correspondent of an Italian newspaper reported. And to make it more easily accessible, the first Venetian public boat service was inaugurated – to Ruskin's fury.[2] He could no longer write in his room at the Hotel Danieli, he said, "because of the accursed whistling of the dirty steam-engine of the omnibus for the Lido." Worse was to follow for by 1881 *vaporetti* were churning up the water of the Grand Canal previously so wonderfully still and silent, troubled only by the splash of the gondoliers' oars. More serious, perhaps, was the resumption of restoration work on San Marco. This met with protests not only from atrabilious foreigners but from many Venetians as well, notably from Ruskin's friend Count Alvise Piero Zorzi. Inside, the pavement of one aisle was completely remade by the English-owned glass-makers, Salviati, in bright new materials. On the façade facing the Piazzetta everything was straightened up, columns and capitals were scraped, old marble slabs and some carvings replaced. And there was a plan afoot to treat the main façade in the same way. Ruskin gave up the struggle

Anonymous, Henry James, c.1880-85

to stay the restorers' hands and concentrated on having photographs and accurate drawings made of what remained untouched.

In a similar spirit, James and other devotees of local colour and pleasing decay cherished all the more fondly the still extensive areas of the city that had been unchanged for decades, or even for centuries. They realized, sadly, that water would eventually be piped to houses and women would no longer fill their pitchers at the beautiful old well-heads all over the city, that mechanization of the glass industry would make the work of bead-stringers obsolete and that the Venetians generally would be better fed and better clothed and no longer provide so distinctive a note of local colour. Though at first James had found them "too squalid and offensive to the nostrils", he now described how they lay in the sunshine, dabbled in the sea, wore their bright rags and fell into attitudes and harmonies. "Not their misery, doubtless, but the way they elude their misery, is what pleases the sentimental tourist, who is gratified by the sight of a beautiful race that lives by the aid of its imagination," especially when posed in front of some "great shabby façade of Gothic windows and balconies – balconies on which dirty clothes are hung

Whistler, San Biagio, 1879-80

and under which a cavernous-looking doorway opens from a low flight of slimy water steps. It is very hot and still, the canal has a queer smell, and the whole place is enchanting." (This might almost be a description of one of Whistler's etchings.)

The room James had taken in 1881 was on the fourth floor of 4161 Riva degli Schiavoni, now the Albergo Paganelli (Castello 4182 and 4687), less than half-way from the Doges' Palace to Whistler's Casa Jankovitz. His window looked out over the

Whistler, The Two Doorways, 1879-80

lagoon and the view was, he said, *"una bellezza"* with the "pink walls of San Giorgio, the downward curve of the Riva, the distant islands, the movement of the quay, the gondolas in profile." Here he wrote every day and finished, or almost finished, *The Portrait of a Lady*. He had a charmed life – "too improbable, too festive", it sometimes seemed to him. He breakfasted every morning at Florian's in Piazza San Marco, before going for a heated salt-water bath at the Stabilimento Chitarin at San Gregorio, near the Salute (recommended by Baedeker and other guide-books). Duly refreshed, he would saunter about the city for an hour or so observing everything, occasionally pausing to admire a church or palace but more often just watching the endless *brio* of Venetian street-life until noon when he took his lunch at Quadri's opposite Florian's in the Piazza. After lunch he returned to his room and worked until six o'clock – or sometimes only until five o'clock so that he might float about in a gondola for a couple of hours before dinner. After dinner he would stroll or just sit at Florian's and listen to the music in the Piazza or, two or three nights a week, call on Mrs Bronson and pass the evening on her balcony, directly opposite the Salute, with, as he later wrote, "its withdrawing rooms behind for more detached conversation; for easy – when not indeed difficult – polyglot talk". There he would meet young Italian naval officers, the Curtises and their guests from further up the Grand Canal, and other "sympathetic *habitués*" of her

Sargent, Venice, 1880-81

little salon, such as Princess Olga, the pathetic, impoverished daughter of the assassinated King Daniel I of Montenegro, in whom he was to become more interested a few years later.[3]

It was not only Mrs Bronson's salon, however, that he recalled when he got back to Bolton Street, London. It had been "a charming time; one of those things that don't repeat themselves", he wrote in his journal.[4] "I seemed to myself to grow young again. The lovely Venetian spring came and went, and brought with it an infinitude of impressions, of delightful hours. I became passionately fond of the place, of the life, of the people, of the habits." A sympathetic, footloose American called Herbert Pratt was there and he remembered "one evening when he took me to a queer little wineshop, haunted only by gondoliers and *facchini*, in an out of the way corner of Venice. We had some excellent muscat wine; he had discovered the place and made himself quite at home there.

Facing page: Whistler, Bead Stringers, 1879-80

Sargent, A Venetian Interior, c.1882

Another evening I went with him to his rooms – far down on the Grand Canal, overlooking the Rialto. It was a hot night; the cry of the gondoliers came up from the canal. He took out a couple of Persian books and read me extracts from Firdausi and Saadi." And these idyllic nights and days came back to him again, with all their intoxicating scents and sounds, when he was writing the preface for a new edition of *The Portrait of a Lady* in 1908: "…the waterside life, the wondrous lagoon spread before me and the ceaseless human chatter of Venice came in at my windows, to which I seem myself to have been constantly driven, in the fruitless fidget of composition, as if to see whether, out in the blue channel, the ship of some right suggestion, of some better phrase, of the next happy twist of my subject, the next true touch for my canvas, mightn't come into sight…"[5] He left in July when the heat became intense. "I left it at last and closed a singularly happy episode; but I took much away with me," he wrote,[6] notably the material for the longest of his essays on the city, published the following November in the *Century Magazine* accompanied by an engraved portrait which he described in a letter to John Addington Symonds as "a horrible effigy of my countenance"[7] and to Isabella Stewart Gardner as "a deformity"[8] done from a "disagreeable photograph". More important, however, were the long-term effects this three months stay were to have on his fiction.

In his mature work – as distinct from such an early story as *The Travelling Companions* – the ambience in which the protagonists confront their ever more complex and more delicately probed moral predicaments is never a merely atmospheric, let alone picturesque, background. It is always a part, an integral part, of the closely woven fabric. And in this increasingly intricate web of motivations and deviations, Venice came to epitomize

Timothy Cole,
Henry James,
(Century Magazine,
November 1882)

Naya studio,
Bead Workers, c.1880

for him the problem confronting many Americans in Europe – the problem of how to reconcile "the delighted senses with the divided, frustrated mind". Venice appears for the first time as a determining force, almost as one of the characters or protagonists of the drama, in *The Princess Casamassima* (published in 1886) – his only political, social-realist novel – in which the proletarian hero Hyacinth Robinson is converted, in Venice, from his revolutionary ideals. The letter which Hyacinth writes from there to the Princess, who has been toying with radical politics, is the turning point in the story:[9] "Want and toil and suffering are the constant lot of the immense majority of the human race," he tells her. "I've found them everywhere here but haven't minded them. Forgive the cynical confession."

As James had written after his last visit, "the misery of Venice stands there for all the world to see; it is part of the spectacle – a thorough-going devotee of local colour might consistently say it was part of the pleasure." And though he distanced himself from his "thorough-going devotee of local colour" he went on to admit, a few lines later, that "it is not easy to say that one would have them [the Venetians] other than they are, and it certainly would make an immense difference should they be better fed." Likewise Hyacinth, under the impact of his first sight of Venice, had come round to a completely apolitical point of view. "What has struck me is the great achievements of which man is capable in spite of them [want and toil and suffering] – the splendid accumulations of the happier few, to which doubtless the miserable many have also in their degree contributed. The face of Europe appears to be covered with them and they've had much the greater part of my attention. They seem to me inestimably precious and beautiful. The monuments and treasures of art, the great palaces and properties, the conquests of learning and taste, the general fabric of civilization as we know it, based if you will upon all the despotisms, the cruelties, the exclusions, the monopolies and the rapacities of the past, but thanks to which, all the same, the world is less of a 'bloody sell' and life more of a lark."

However, the sharply focused descriptions of "this incomparable

James Craig Annan,
Campo S. Margherita,
1896

abominable old Venice" which follow in Hyacinth Robinson's letter are not, as
one might expect, of its great and noble buildings and monuments and works
of art: they are glimpses of picturesque local life in the back alleys such as
Whistler and Sargent had painted. "I have a room in a little *campo* opposite a
small old church which has cracked marble slabs let into the front; and in the
cracks grow little wild delicate flowers of which I don't know the name. Over the
door of the church hangs an old battered leather curtain, polished and tawny,
as thick as a mattress and with buttons in it like a sofa; and it flops to and fro
laboriously as women and girls, with shawls on their heads and their feet in
little wooden shoes which have nothing but toes, pass in and out. In the middle
of the *campo* is a fountain that looks still older than the church; it has a primitive
barbaric air, and I've an idea it was put there by the first settlers – those who
came to Venice from the mainland, from Aquileia. I bend a genial eye on the

*Sargent, Venetian Water
Carriers, c.1882*

James Craig Annan,
A Beggar, 1896

women and girls I just spoke of as they glide with a small clatter and with their old copper water-jars to the fountain. The Venetian girl-face is wonderfully sweet and the effect is charming when its pale sad oval (they all look underfed) is framed in the old faded shawl. They have also the most engaging hair, which has never done curling, and they slip along together, in couples and threes, interlinked by the arms and never meeting one's eye – so that its geniality doesn't matter – dressed in thin cheap cotton gowns whose limp folds make the same delightful line that everything in Italy makes. The weather is splendid and I roast – but I like it; apparently I was made to be spitted and 'done' and I discovered that I've been cold all my life even when I thought I was warm. I've seen none of the beautiful patricians who sat for the great painters – the gorgeous beings whose golden hair was intertwined with pearls; but I'm studying Italian in order to talk with the shuffling clicking maidens who work in the bead-factories – I'm determined to make one or two of them look at me. When they've filled their old water-pots at the fountain it's jolly to see them perch them on their heads and patter away over the polished Venetian stones. The floor of my room is composed of little brick tiles, and to freshen the air in this temperature one sprinkles it, as you no doubt know, with water. Before long if I keep sprinkling I shall be able to swim about; the green shutters are closed and the place makes a very good tank. Through the chinks the hot light of the *campo* comes in. I smoke cigarettes and in the pauses of this composition recline on a faded magenta divan in the corner. When I've finished this I shall go forth and wander about in the splendid Venetian afternoon; and I shall spend the evening in that enchanted square of St Mark's which resembles an immense open-air drawing room, listening to music and feeling the sea-breeze blow in between those two strange old columns of the Piazzetta which seem to make a doorway for it."

James returned to Venice twice in 1887, as if to make up for the six years that had passed since his previous visit. From 22nd February to 16th April he stayed with Mrs Bronson in her *foresteria* or guest-house at the back of Ca' Alvisi – "a very snug and comfortable little apartment of several rooms".[10] His hostess was, he wrote, "a most benevolent, injudiciously (even) generous woman, adored by all the common people of Venice – and preyed upon by her servants." Her salon, which had been James's great social resource when last in Venice, could now boast of Sir Henry Layard (discoverer of Nineveh) and his wife, who had recently bought Ca' Capello further up the Grand Canal; Prince Paul Metternich (son of the Austrian statesman who had been hated by all Italian patriots); Don Carlos (pretender to the Spanish throne) and various ageing relics of the Venetian patrician families. James kept his distance from them, despite their links with the past, except for the Contessa Evelyn Pisani. She fascinated him: widow of the last descendant of an early eighteenth-century Doge and numerous high officials of the Serene Republic – and also a link with the "gorgeous East" that Venice had once held "in fee", for her father had been the English doctor who bled Byron to death at Missolonghi and then settled in Constantinople where he became court physician to a succession of five Sultans. Her mother, at one time married to an Effendi, was whispered to have been – as James believed – "a French *odalisque* out of the harem of the Grand Turk".[11] With this romantic past Contessa Pisani was "widowed, childless, palaced, villaed, pictured, jewelled and modified by Venetian society in a kind of mysterious awe." Most of her time was spent on her country estate which , as a devotee of Edward Lear, she re-named Gromboolia – it was to be charmingly described by Margaret Symonds (daughter of James's friend James Addington Symonds) in *Days Spent on a Doge's Farm*. She was also the sitting tenant on the mezzanine floor of Palazzo Barbaro which had first been rented by the Curtises and then bought by them in December 1885.

There was a friendly rivalry between the Curtises and Mrs Bronson for the leadership of American-Venetian society – Lady Layard being the Queen of Anglo-Venetian society – and this raged especially over the poor, frail but still irrepressible Robert Browning who read his poems to select gatherings in both Ca' Alvisi and Palazzo Barbaro. Vernon Lee, who was introduced to the Curtises through Sargent, found them "most friendly and amiable"[12] and the Palazzo Barbaro "a vast and luxurious and exquisite place, full of beautiful furniture and pictures and at the same time absolutely unpretentious". Daniel Curtis, she remarked, "is a nice brisk little man, rather timidly anxious to put in a little piece of information or an anecdote or joke here and there; his wife is of the rather die-away English American, and is pathetic over the omnibus steamers which ply up and down the Grand Canal; but she is also very amiable. These sort of Americans, who shudder at Howells, look up to James as a sort of patron saint of cosmopolitan refinement." James, who never suffered bores

Naya studio, Rio Marin with Ca' Capello on the left, c.1890

gladly, was rather more pointed in his remarks about Daniel Curtis – "one calculates the time when one shall have worked through his anecdotes and come out the other side. Perhaps one never does – it is an unboreable – or unbearable – St Gothard."[13] Curtis was doing his best "to make the Grand Canal seem like Beacon Street", the citadel of Boston Brahmins. Returning to Venice in June, however, when Mrs Bronson had gone to her summer retreat at Asolo – "one of the quaintest possible little places of *villeggiatura*", James called it – he went to stay with the Curtises in their "magnificent old Palace – all marble, and frescoes and portraits of Doges – a delightful habitation for hot weather"[14] which he found altogether most sympathetic. And here he completed *The Aspern Papers*, his only fiction entirely set in Venice.

Early that year in Florence, James had heard, from Vernon Lee's half-brother,[15] the story of an American who had discovered that Claire Claremont was still living there and schemed to obtain the letters she had received from Byron and Shelley but, after her death, fled when offered them by her middle-aged niece on the condition that he marry her. It was too good a subject to miss and James set to work almost at once. But he transformed Byron-Shelley into a fictitious American poet, Jeffrey Aspern, and shifted the scene to Venice – there being, as he was later to explain, "no refinement of the mouldy rococo, in human form, that you may not disembark at the dislocated water-steps of almost any decayed monument of Venetian greatness in suspicious quest of."[16]

The house he had in mind was the seventeenth-century Ca' Capello on Rio Marin which leads out of the Grand Canal opposite the church of the Scalzi (near the railway station and much less remote than James suggests in the story, though of course less prominent than the Layards' Ca' Capello on the Grand Canal). James knew it as the home of his expatriate American friends Constance Fletcher,[17] her aged mother and the painter Eugene Benson. Constance was a writer who had scored an early success with a sensational best-seller *Kismet. A Nile Novel* (1877), wrote plays and contributed to the *Yellow Book* under the pseudonym of George Fleming. She was also the possessor of letters from and a portrait miniature of Byron (sought after by numerous collectors) which she had been given by his grandson, Lord Lovelace, to whom she was briefly engaged to be married – a connection with the Romantic past which made Ca' Capello peculiarly appropriate as the setting for *The Aspern Papers*. The household was, furthermore, viewed askance by fashionable American society for Mrs Fletcher was known to have fallen in love with her son's English tutor, left her husband and gone to Europe where she finally settled down with Eugene Benson (whether or not they ever married is uncertain). James had known Benson since 1872 in Rome and Benson was perhaps the "original" for Singleton in *Roderick Hudson*.

Venice living tenaciously on its past, in fragile beauty perpetually threatened by the intrusion of modernity, was more than a mere setting for this story of privacy brashly invaded to possess the secrets of a romantic passion. The city is part of the tale and the gentle lapping of water on stone in the wake of a gondola's gliding movement echoes through its pages. With glancing touches, as deft and subtle as those of Whistler's pastels, James evoked the atmosphere of secluded back-canals flanked by dilapidated, apparently deserted buildings whose shuttered windows suggest, while protecting from prying eyes, a mysterious life in death. "The gondola stopped, the old palace was there,"[18] the narrator recalls; "it was a house of the class which in Venice carries even in extreme dilapidation the dignified name. 'How charming! It's grey and pink' my companion exclaimed; and that is the most comprehensive description of it. It was not particularly old, only two or three centuries; and it had an air not so much of decay as of quiet discouragement, as if it had rather missed its career. But its wide front, with a stone balcony from end to end of the *piano nobile* or most important floor, was architectural enough, with the aid of various pilasters and arches; and the stucco with which in the intervals it had long ago been endued was rosy in the April afternoon. It overlooked a clean melancholy rather lonely canal, which had a narrow riva or convenient footway on either side." A high blank wall "appeared to confine an expanse of ground on one side of the house. Blank I call it, but it was figured over with the patches that please a painter, repaired breaches, crumblings of plaster, extrusions of brick that had turned pink with time; while the few thin trees, with the poles of certain rickety trellises, were visible over the top. The place was a garden and apparently attached to the house." The narrator is admitted, follows a servant as "she pattered across the damp stony lower hall" and "up the high staircase – stonier still, as it seemed," to the *sala*.[19] "It had a gloomy grandeur, but owed its character almost all to its noble shape and fine architectural doors, as high as those of grand frontages, which, leading into various rooms, repeated themselves on either side at intervals. They were surmounted with old faded

Sargent, Venetian Interior, c. 1882

painted escutcheons, and here and there in the spaces between them hung brown pictures, which I noted as speciously bad, in battered and tarnished frames that were yet more desirable than the canvases themselves. With the exception of several straw-bottomed chairs that kept their backs to the wall the grand obscure vista contained little else to minister to effect." Was James describing an interior he had seen? Or a painting by Sargent? Another great empty *sala* was the setting for the climactic scene in a slightly later short story, *The Pupil*. "One sad November day, while the wind roared round the old palace and the rain lashed the lagoon," the tutor, Pemberton, "walked up and down the big bare *sala* with his pupil. The *scagliola* floor was cold, the high battered casements shook in the storm, and the stately decay of the place was unrelieved by a particle of furniture."[20]

In *The Aspern Papers*, the remote water-way on which the Misses Bordereau's palace stands, is contrasted with the splendour of the Grand Canal on a clear summer evening, when "the sense of floating between marble palaces and reflected lights disposed the mind to freedom and ease"[21] and the "splendid square which serves as a vast forecourt to the strange old church of St Mark", called up, it would seem, fond recollections of all the evenings he had spent there since his first visit in 1869: "in front of Florian's café eating ices, listening to music, talking with acquaintances: the traveller will remember how the immense cluster of tables and little chairs stretches like a promontory into the smooth lake of the Piazza. The whole place, of a summer's evening, under the stars and with all the lamps, all the voices and light footsteps on marble – the only sounds of the immense arcade that encloses it – is an open-air saloon dedicated to cooling drinks and to a still finer degustation, that of the splendid impressions received during the day. When I didn't prefer to keep mine to myself there was always a stray tourist, disencumbered of his Baedeker, to discuss them with, or some domesticated painter rejoicing in the return of the season of strong effects. The great basilica, with its mosaic and sculpture, looked ghostly in the tempered gloom, and the sea-breeze passed between the twin columns of the Piazzetta, the lintels of a door no longer guarded, as gently as if a rich curtain swayed there."[22]

When the air is not "aglow with the sunset" it seems already to be night-time in this evocation of Venice, as in so many of Whistler's paintings, pastels and etchings. "The place was hushed and void; the quiet neighbourhood had gone to sleep. A lamp, here and there, over the narrow black water, glimmered in double; the voice of a man going homeward singing, his jacket on his shoulder and his hat on his ear, came to us from a distance. Presently a gondola passed along the canal with its slow rhythmical plash, and as we listened we watched in silence."[23] There is little noise in the city at any time, "without streets and vehicles, the uproar of the wheels, the brutality of horses" – only the distant sound of walkers "clicking over bridges". And except in the Piazza there are few people. Apart from the two Misses Bordereau and their inconspicuous cook the only characters in *The Aspern Papers* are the narrator's hostess Mrs Prest (a barely disguised portrait of Mrs Bronson) and his gondolier whose betrothed is "a young lady with powdered face, a yellow cotton gown and much leisure" who, almost inevitably, "practised at her convenience the art of a stringer of beads."

In June 1890 James spent a fortnight in Palazzo Barbaro. "Venice continues adorable and the Curtises the soul of benevolence," he told his sister.[24] "Their upstairs apartment (empty and still unoffered – at forty pounds a year – to anyone but me) beckons me so as a foot-in-the-water here, and if my dramatic ship had begun to come in, I should probably be tempted to take it at a venture – for all it would matter. But for the present I resist perfectly – especially as Venice isn't *all* advantageous. The great charm of such an idea is the having in Italy, a little cheap and private refuge independent of hotels etc. which every

Whistler, Riva Sunset: Red and Gold, 1879-80

Whistler, Nocturne: Palaces, from "The Second Venice Set", 1879-80

year grow more disagreeable and German and tiresome to face – not to say dearer too."

So his interest in the English and American residents' "Palazzo-madness", as he called it, was tempered – even when the vast Palazzo Rezzonico was bought by Robert Browning's unsatisfactory son "Pen" – "halfpenny Browning he ought to be called", according to Ralph Curtis. Browning himself had been dubious about the purchase: "don't be a little man in a big house," he told his son. Meeting James in London in 1888, Browning talked of Venice and, as always, told James "the same thing – that the 'dealers' have offered Pen the eyes of their head for the mere superogatory fixtures of his disproportionate palace. And Pen is sketched with paternal fondness as making a kind of *pied de nez*."[25] Browning was to spend his last months in Palazzo Rezzonico, dying there in December 1889. James went the following year and reported that what Pen had done "through his American wife's dollars ... transcends description for the beauty, and, as Ruskin would say, 'wisdom and rightness' of it. It is altogether royal and imperial – but 'Pen' isn't kingly and the *train de vie* remains to be seen. Gondoliers ushering in friends from pensions won't fill it out."[26] The bare rooms which Whistler, Sargent, Boldini and other artists had rented as studios were now lavishly furnished. And as if the ceilings frescoed by Tiepolo on the *piano nobile* were not enough, Pen painted others on the floor above. "Poor grotesque little Pen – and poor sacrificed little Mrs P," James was to write in 1893.[27] "There seems but one way to be sane in this queer world – but there are so many ways of being mad. And a Palazzo-madness is almost as alarming – or as convulsive – as an earthquake – which indeed it essentially resembles."

However, he had felt no such qualms when invited to spend July in Venice *en grand luxe* as the

Anonymous, Robert and Pen Browning, Venice, c.1889

Anders Zorn, Isabella Stewart Gardner, 1894

Joseph Lindon Smith, Cortile of Palazzo Barbaro, c.1894

Anonymous, Mrs Gardner and gondolier, Venice, c.1894

guest of the already celebrated American millionairess art-collector and hostess, Isabella Stewart Gardner – "Mrs Jack" or "Boston's first, pre-cinema star" as Berenson was to call her – who had rented the Palazzo Barbaro from the Curtises for the summer of 1892 as she was to do almost every other summer for many years.

She was an old friend of James and of the Curtises – Ralph had introduced her to Sargent who painted his famous portrait of her, wearing her strings of pearls with ruby pendants, standing in front of a splendid piece of Venetian velvet[28] – and Palazzo Barbaro with its sumptuous gilded and stuccoed rooms behind a crumbling Gothic façade captivated her. The *cortile*, in which she took her Italian lessons every day, was to inspire the Venetian Gothic central interior courtyard, glazed overhead and festooned with hanging nasturtiums, of her Fenway Court in Boston. It was depicted by one of her favourite protégés, Joseph Lindon Smith whom she nick-named "Colli" because she had "discovered" him drawing the head of Verrochio's equestrian statue of Colleoni. In Venice she assembled an international circle of artists and musicians, one of whom – the Swedish painter Anders Zorn – portrayed her as she appeared one night in that state of almost continual over-excitement that so amused her guests, bursting into the great *sala* of Palazzo Barbaro from the balcony overlooking the Grand Canal and summoning everyone to watch a firework display. James recorded how, one morning, he was in attendance as she sat with her "hair not quite up – neither up nor down, as it were, in a gauze dressing gown on a sea-green (so different from pea-green!) chair beneath a glorious gilded ceiling, receiving the matutinal tea from a Venetian slave."[29] The house was so full of guests that he was given as a bedroom the "divine old library", stretching the whole depth of the building on the top floor. "Have you ever lived here?" he asked Ariana Curtis.[30] "If you haven't, if you haven't gazed upward from your couch, in the rosy dawn, or during the postprandial (that is after luncheon) siesta, at the medallions and arabesques of the ceiling, permit me to tell you that you don't *know* the Barbaro. Let me add that I am not here in wantonness or disorder – but simply because the little lady's other boarders are located elsewhere. I am so far from complaining that "I wish I could stay here for ever."

A curious counterpart to James's accounts of his life in Venice at this time was given by Vernon Lee in a story, *Lady Tal*, published before the end of 1892.[31] Its setting cannot be mistaken. "The church of the Salute, with its cupolas and volutes, stared in at the long windows, white, luminous, spectral. A white carpet of moonlight stretched to where they were sitting, with only one lamp lit, for fear of mosquitoes. All the remoter parts of the vast drawing room were deep in gloom; you were somehow conscious of the paintings and stuccoes of the walls without seeing them." The assembled company might have been encountered either in Palazzo Barbaro or Ca' Alvisi: it includes "the old peeress, her head tied up in a white pocket-handkerchief … the American Senator seated with a postage stamp profile and the attitude of a bronze statesman … the depressed Venetian naval officer who always made the little joke about not being ill when offered tea … the Roumanian Princess who cultivated the reputation of saying spiteful things cleverly, and wore all her pearls for fear of their tarnishing." The description of the hostess "whose round, unchangeable face, the face of a world-wise, kind but somewhat frivolous baby" recalls the Ariana Curtis of Sargent's *An Interior in Venice* (see p.146). And there can be no doubt that Henry James was the original for the main character, Jervase Marion, an expatriate American novelist living in London who is inveigled by Lady Tal into helping her with a novel she is writing, with a suggestion of further and closer collaboration. On the first page he appears lolling on an ottoman: "that lolling of his always struck one as out of keeping with his well-adjusted speech, his precise mind, the something conventional about him." He has not only James's well-known manner of talking with many hesitations, and his "little frown as if his boot pinched" but also his "habit of studying people, of turning them round, prodding and cutting them to see what was inside" combined with his "tendency to withdraw from all personal concerns, from all emotion or action." William James found the portrayal of his brother "clever enough" and "not exactly malicious". But Henry, who claimed that he had not read this "satire of a flagrant and markedly 'saucy' kind," was deeply and unforgivingly offended. And the Americans in Venice at once closed ranks, barring their doors against Vernon Lee. The only member of their circle who remained on friendly terms with her was Sargent.

Anonymous,
The Gardners and the
Zorns, Venice, 1894

Böhm studio, The Salone,
Palazzo Barbaro, c.1900

*Böhm studio, The Library,
Palazzo Barbaro, c.1900*

Little more than a year later, James found himself caught in a situation far more serious and painful than that imagined by Vernon Lee. In January 1894 news reached him in London of the death in Venice of the American novelist Constance Fenimore Woolson (grandniece of Fenimore Cooper). They had struck up a friendship soon after she arrived in London in 1880, met frequently in England, Italy and Switzerland and wrote regularly to each other. She looked after him when he succumbed briefly to jaundice in Venice in 1887 and a year later his sister Alice reported that he was "somewhere on the Continent flirting with Constance".[32] When she was ill in Oxford in 1892 he went to see her assiduously. Clearly, she thought of him as more than just a friend and, in fact, became deeply attached to him. The following year she took an apartment in Venice and James promised to visit her. But for him, with his large acquaintance, she was only one of many dear friends.

She had committed suicide by throwing herself from a window on the top floor of Casa Semitecolo on the Grand Canal. James was horrified. He had known her so long. He was convulsed with grief – and by twinges of remorse and even, perhaps, of guilt. "Horror stricken," he wrote, "sickened by the news – too haunted with the image of the act" to face the prospect of attending her funeral.[33] During the following weeks James tried to convince himself that he could have done nothing to avert the tragedy. She had for so long been isolated by deafness and, although successful as a popular novelist, increasingly subject to fits of depression. But he only too clearly revealed, in his attempts to exorcise it, the suspicion that he might, in the gallantry of his conversation and the effusion of his letters, have encouraged an affection he was unable to return and had, unknowingly and continually, rebuffed. On 2nd February he wrote to Mrs Bronson: "I can't, while the freshness of such a misery as it all must have been is in the air, feel anything but that Venice is not a place I want immediately to see."[34] And yet, little more than a month later, a "combination of circumstances",[35] as he put it in a letter

*Anonymous,
Henry James's bed in the
library, 1892*

to Mrs Bronson, "make it absolutely necessary I should be in Venice from the 1st April. This being the case, as I have work in hand, I must get into some quiet and comfortable material conditions – and I particularly detest the Venetian hotels: loathe in fact to be in a hotel, in Venice, even for a day. It occurs to me that the apartment occupied by Miss Woolson last summer before she went to Casa Semitecolo and which I believe she found very comfortable, may be free and obtainable." Arrangements were thus made for him to take the very rooms Fenimore Woolson had had shortly before moving to the nearby house where she committed suicide.

James went to Venice, ostensibly, to help Fenimore Woolson's sister sort out the dead woman's possessions: but he probably had other motives, as well – to ensure, perhaps, that no compromising letters or other documents should fall into the hands of such a "publishing scoundrel" as the narrator in *The Aspern Papers*. And, in fact, he appears to have found in Venice, and destroyed, all his letters to Fenimore Woolson. Her other belongings were packed up and sent to America. But for some reason it was decided that her clothing should be disposed of in the lagoon. "There were a lot of clothes, a lot

Whistler, Little Venice, 1879-80

of black dresses" he told a friend who, many years later, recorded the account James had given her: "…he threw them in the water and they came up like balloons around him, and the more he tried to throw them down, they got all this air, the more they came up and he was surrounded by these horrible black balloons … he kept on saying … he tried to beat these horrible black things down and up they came again and he was surrounded by them."[36] It was as if some long suppressed fears and doubts – his dark thoughts – had at last forced themselves up to the surface of his mind. He could repress them no longer.

He tried to stay on in Venice for a while but soon fled to Rome and then to Florence. When he returned he wrote to Mrs Gardner to tell her that he would not be able to join her court that summer at Palazzo Barbaro.[37] Indeed he was not sure whether he would ever return to Venice again.

FOUR ESSAYS

from

ITALIAN HOURS

by

HENRY JAMES

VENICE

It is a great pleasure to write the word; but I am not sure there is not a certain impudence in pretending to add anything to it. Venice has been painted and described many thousands of times, and of all the cities of the world is the easiest to visit without going there. Open the first book and you will find a rhapsody about it; step into the first picture-dealer's and you will find three or four high-coloured "views" of it. There is notoriously nothing more to be said on the subject. Every one has been there, and every one has brought back a collection of photographs. There is as little mystery about the Grand Canal as about our local thoroughfare, and the name of St Mark is as familiar as the postman's ring. It is not forbidden, however, to speak of familiar things, and I hold that for the true Venice-lover Venice is always in order. There is nothing new to be said about her certainly, but the old is better than any novelty. It would be a sad day indeed when there should be something new to say. I write these lines with the full consciousness of having no information whatever to offer. I do not pretend to enlighten the reader; I pretend only to give a fillip to his memory; and I hold any writer sufficiently justified who is himself in love with his theme.

Whistler, Nocturne, from "The First Venice Set", 1879-80

91

I

Mr Ruskin has given it up, that is very true; but only after extracting half a lifetime of pleasure and an immeasurable quantity of fame from it. We all may do the same, after it has served our turn, which it probably will not cease to do for many a year to come. Meantime it is Mr Ruskin who beyond any one helps us to enjoy. He has indeed lately produced several aids to depression in the shape of certain little humorous – ill-humorous – pamphlets (the series of *St Mark's Rest*) which embody his latest reflections on the subject of our city and describe the latest atrocities perpetrated there. These latter are numerous and deeply to be deplored; but to admit that they have spoiled Venice would be to admit that Venice may be spoiled – an admission pregnant, as it seems to us, with disloyalty. Fortunately one reacts against the Ruskinian contagion, and one hour of the lagoon is worth a hundred pages of demoralised prose. This queer late-coming prose of Mr Ruskin (including the revised and condensed issue of the *Stones of Venice*, only one little volume of which has been published, or perhaps ever will be) is all to be read, though much of it appears addressed to children of tender age. It is pitched in the nursery-key, and might be supposed to emanate from an angry governess. It is, however, all suggestive, and much of it is delightfully just. There is an inconceivable want of form in it, though the author has spent his life in laying down the principles of form and scolding people for departing from them; but it throbs and flashes with the love of his subject – a love disconcerted and abjured, but which has still much of the force of inspiration. Among the many strange things that have befallen Venice, she has had the good fortune to become the object of a passion to a man of splendid genius, who has made her his own and in doing so has made her the world's. There is no better reading at Venice therefore, as I say, than Ruskin, for every true Venice-lover can separate the wheat from the chaff. The narrow theological spirit, the moralism *à tout propos*, the queer provincialities and pruderies, are mere wild weeds in a mountain of flowers. One may doubtless be very happy in Venice without

Naya studio, San Trovaso, c.1880

reading at all – without criticising or analysing or thinking a strenuous thought. It is a city in which, I suspect, there is very little strenuous thinking, and yet it is a city in which there must be almost as much happiness as misery. The misery of Venice stands there for all the world to see; it is part of the spectacle – a thorough-going devotee of local colour might consistently say it is part of the pleasure. The Venetian people have little to call their own – little more than the bare privilege of leading their lives in the most beautiful of towns. Their habitations are decayed; their taxes heavy; their pockets light; their opportunities few. One receives an impression, however, that life presents itself to them with attractions not accounted for in this meagre train of advantages, and that they are on better terms with it than many people who have made a better bargain. They lie in the sunshine; they dabble in the sea; they wear bright rags; they fall into attitudes and harmonies; they assist at an eternal *conversazione*. It is not easy to say that one would have them other than they are, and it certainly would make an immense difference should they be better fed. The number of persons in Venice who evidently never have enough to eat is painfully large; but it would be more painful if we did not equally perceive that the rich Venetian temperament may bloom upon a dog's allowance. Nature has been kind to it, and sunshine and leisure and conversation and beautiful views form the greater part of its sustenance. It takes a great deal to make a successful American, but to make a happy Venetian takes only a handful of quick sensibility. The Italian people have at once the good and the evil fortune to be conscious of few wants; so that if the civilisation of a society is measured by the number of its needs, as seems to be the common opinion today, it is to be feared that the children of the lagoon would make but a poor figure in a set of comparative tables. Not their misery, doubtless, but the way they elude their misery, is what pleases the sentimental tourist, who is gratified by the sight of a beautiful race that lives by the aid of its imagination. The way to enjoy Venice is to follow the example of these people and make the most of simple pleasures. Almost all the pleasures of the place are simple; this may be maintained even under the imputation of ingenious paradox. There is no simpler pleasure than looking at a fine Titian, unless it be looking at a fine Tintoret or strolling into St Mark's – abominable the way one falls into the habit – and resting one's light-wearied eyes upon the windowless gloom; or than floating in a gondola or than hanging over a balcony or than taking one's coffee at Florian's. It is of such superficial pastimes that a Venetian day is composed, and the pleasure of the matter is in the emotions to which they minister. These are fortunately of the finest – otherwise Venice would be insufferably dull. Reading Ruskin is good; reading the old records is perhaps better; but the best thing of all is simply staying on. The only way to care for Venice as she deserves it is to give her a chance to touch you often – to linger and remain and return.

II

The danger is that you will not linger enough – a danger of which the author of these lines had known something. It is possible to dislike Venice, and to entertain the sentiment in a responsible and intelligent manner. There are travellers who think the place odious, and those who are not of this opinion often find themselves wishing that

the others were only more numerous. The sentimental tourist's sole quarrel with his Venice is that he has too many competitors there. He likes to be alone; to be original; to have (to himself, at least) the air of making discoveries. The Venice of today is a vast museum where the little wicket that admits you is perpetually turning and creaking, and you march through the institution with a herd of fellow-gazers. There is nothing left to discover or describe, and originality of attitude is

Whistler, Bead Stringing, Venice, 1879-80

Sargent, A Street in Venice, 1882

completely impossible. This is often very annoying; you can only turn your back on your impertinent playfellow and curse his want of delicacy. But this is not the fault of Venice; it is the fault of the rest of the world. The fault of Venice is that, though she is easy to admire, she is not so easy to live with as you count living in other places. After you have stayed a week and the bloom of novelty has rubbed off you wonder if you can accommodate yourself to the peculiar conditions. Your old habits become impracticable and you find yourself obliged to form new ones of an undesirable and unprofitable character. You are tired of your gondola (or you think you are) and you have seen all the principal pictures and heard the names of the palaces announced a dozen times by your gondolier, who brings them out almost as impressively as if he were an English butler bawling titles into a drawing-room. You have walked several hundred times round the Piazza and bought several bushels of photographs. You have visited the antiquity-mongers whose horrible sign-boards dishonour some of the grandest vistas in the Grand Canal; you have tried the opera and found it very bad; you have bathed at the Lido and found the water flat. You have begun to have a shipboard-feeling – to regard the Piazza as an enormous saloon and the Riva degli Schiavoni as a promenade-deck. You are obstructed and encaged; your desire for space is unsatisfied; you miss your usual exercise. You try to take a walk and you fail, and meantime, as I say, you have come to regard your gondola as a sort of magnified baby's cradle. You have no desire to be rocked to sleep, though you are sufficiently kept awake by the irritation produced, as you gaze across the shallow lagoon, by the attitude of the perpetual gondolier, with his turned-out toes, his protruded chin, his absurdly unscientific stroke. The canals have a horrible smell, and the everlasting Piazza, where you have looked repeatedly at every article in every shop-window and found them all rubbish, where the young Venetians who sell bead bracelets and "panoramas" are perpetually thrusting their wares at you, where the same tightly-buttoned officers are for ever sucking the same black weeds, at the same empty tables, in front of the same cafés – the Piazza, as I say, has resolved itself into a magnificent tread-mill. This is the state of mind of those shallow enquirers who find Venice all very well for a week; and if in such a state of mind you take your departure you act with fatal rashness. The loss is your own, moreover; it is not – with all deference to your personal attractions – that of your companions who remain behind; for though there are some disagreeable things in Venice there is nothing so disagreeable as the visitors. The conditions are peculiar, but your intolerance of them evaporates before it has had time to become a prejudice. When you have called for the bill to go, pay it and remain, and you will find on the morrow that you are deeply attached to Venice. It is by living there from day to day that you feel the fullness of her charm; that you invite her exquisite influence to sink into your spirit. The creature varies like a nervous woman, whom you know only when you know all the aspects of her beauty. She has high spirits or low, she is pale or red, grey or pink, cold or warm, fresh or wan, according to the weather or the hour. She is always interesting and almost always sad; but she has a thousand occasional graces and is always liable to happy accidents. You become extraordinarily fond of these things; you count upon them; they make part of your life. Tenderly fond you become; there is something indefinable in those depths of personal acquaintance that gradually establish themselves. The place seems to personify itself, to become human and sentient and conscious of your affection. You desire to embrace it, to caress it, to possess it; and finally a soft sense of possession grows up and your visit becomes a perpetual love-affair. It is very true that if you go, as the author of these lines on a certain occasion went, about the middle of March, a certain amount of disappointment is possible. He had paid no visit for several years, and in the interval the beautiful and helpless city had suffered an increase of injury. The barbarians are in full possession and you tremble for what they may do. You are reminded from the moment of your arrival that Venice scarcely exists any more as a city at all; that she exists only as a battered peep-show and bazaar. There was a horde of savage Germans encamped in the Piazza, and they filled the Ducal Palace and the Academy with their uproar. The English and Americans came a little later. They came in good time, with a great many French, who were discreet enough to make very long repasts at the Caffè Quadri, during which they were out of the way. The months of April and May of the year 1881 were not, as a general thing, a favourable season for visiting the Ducal Palace and the Academy. The *valet-de-place* had marked them for his own and held triumphant possession of them. He celebrates his triumphs in a terrible brassy voice, which resounds all over the place, and has, whatever language he be speaking, the accent of some other idiom. During all the spring months in Venice these gentry abound in the great resorts, and they lead their helpless captives through churches and galleries in dense irresponsible groups. They infest the Piazza; they pursue you along the Riva; they hang about the bridges and the doors of the cafés. In saying just now that I was disappointed at first, I had chiefly in mind the impression that assails me today in the whole precinct of St Mark's. The condition of this ancient sanctuary is surely a great scandal. The pedlars and commissioners ply their trade – often a very unclean one – at the very door of the temple; they follow you across the threshold, into the sacred dusk, and pull your sleeve, and hiss into your ear, scuffling with each other for customers. There is a great deal of dishonour about St Mark's altogether, and if Venice, as I say, has become a great bazaar, this exquisite edifice is now the biggest booth.

III

It is treated as a booth in all ways, and if it had not somehow a great spirit of solemnity within it the traveller would soon have little warrant for regarding it as a religious affair. The restoration of the outer walls, which has lately been so much attacked and defended, is certainly a great shock. Of the necessity of the work only an expert is, I suppose, in a position to judge; but there is no doubt that, if a necessity it be, it is one that is deeply to be regretted. To no more distressing necessity have people

of taste lately had to resign themselves. Wherever the hand of the restorer has been laid all semblance of beauty has vanished; which is a sad fact, considering that the external loveliness of St Mark's has been for ages less impressive only than that of the still comparatively uninjured interior. I know not what is the measure of necessity in such a case, and it appears indeed to be a very delicate question. Today, at any rate, that admirable harmony of faded mosaic and marble which, to the eye of the traveller emerging from the narrow streets that lead to the Piazza, filled all the further end of it with a sort of dazzling silvery presence – today this lovely vision is in a way to be completely reformed and indeed well-nigh abolished. The old softness and mellowness of colour – the work of the quiet centuries and of the breath of the salt sea – is giving way to large crude patches of new material which have the effect of a monstrous malady rather than of a restoration to health. They look like blotches of red and white paint and dishonourable smears of chalk on the cheeks of a noble matron. The face toward the Piazzetta is in especial the newest-looking thing conceivable – as new as a new pair of boots or as the morning's paper. We do not profess, however, to undertake a scientific quarrel with these changes; we admit that our complaint is a purely sentimental one. The march of industry in united Italy must doubtless be looked at as a whole, and one must endeavour to believe that it is through innumerable lapses of taste that this deeply interesting country is groping her way to her place among the nations. For the present, it is not to be denied, certain odd phases of the process are more visible than the result, to arrive at which it seems necessary that, as she was of old a passionate votary of the beautiful, she should today burn everything that she has adored. It is doubtless too soon to judge her, and there are moments when one is willing to forgive her even the restoration of St Mark's. Inside as well there has been a considerable attempt to make the place more tidy; but the general effect, as yet, has not seriously suffered. What I chiefly remember is the straightening out of that dark and rugged old pavement – those deep undulations of primitive

Whistler, The Piazzetta, 1879-80

mosaic in which the fond spectator was thought to perceive an intended resemblance to the waves of the ocean. Whether intended or not the analogy was an image the more in a treasure-house of images; but from a considerable portion of the church it has now disappeared. Throughout the greater part indeed the pavement remains as recent generations have known it – dark, rich, cracked, uneven, spotted with porphyry and time-blackened malachite, polished by the knees of innumerable worshippers; but in other large stretches the idea imitated by the restorers is that of the ocean in a dead calm, and the model they have taken the floor of a London club-house or of a New York hotel. I think no Venetian and scarcely any Italian cares much for such differences; and when, a year ago, people in England were writing to *The Times* about the whole business and holding meetings to protest against it the dear children of the lagoon – so far as they heard or heeded the rumour – thought them partly busy-bodies and partly asses. Busy-bodies they doubtless were, but they took a good deal of disinterested trouble. It never occurs to the Venetian mind of today that such trouble may be worth taking; the Venetian mind vainly endeavours to conceive a state of existence in which personal questions are so insipid that people have to look for grievances in the wrongs of brick and marble. I must not, however, speak of St Mark's as if I had the pretension of giving a description of it or as if the reader desired one. The reader has been too well served already. It is surely the best-described building in the world. Open the *Stones of Venice*, open Théophile Gautier's *Italia*, and you will see. These writers take it very seriously, and it is only because there is another way of taking it that I venture to speak of it; the way that offers itself after you have been in Venice a couple of months, and the light is hot in the great Square, and you pass in under the pictured porticoes with a feeling of habit and friendliness and a desire for something cool and dark. There are moments, after all, when the church is comparatively quiet and empty, and when you may sit there with an easy consciousness of its beauty. From the moment, of course, that you go into any Italian church for any purpose

Sargent, The Pavement, Venice, 1898

but to say your prayers or look at the ladies, you rank yourself among the trooping barbarians I just spoke of; you treat the place as an orifice in the peep-show. Still, it is almost a spiritual function – or, at the worst, an amorous one – to feed one's eyes on the molten colour that drops from the hollow vaults and thickens the air with its richness. It is all so quiet and sad and faded and yet all so brilliant and living. The strange figures in the mosaic pictures, bending with the curve of niche and vault, stare down through the glowing dimness; the burnished gold that stands behind them catches the light on its little uneven cubes. St Mark's owes nothing of its character to the beauty of proportion or perspective; there is nothing grandly balanced or far-arching; there are no long lines nor triumphs of the perpendicular. The church arches indeed, but arches like a dusky cavern. Beauty of surface, of tone, of detail, of things near enough to touch and kneel upon and lean against – it is from this the effect proceeds. In this sort of beauty the place is incredibly rich, and you may go there every day and find afresh some lurking pictorial nook. It is a treasury of bits, as the painters say; and there are usually three or four of the fraternity with their easels set up in uncertain equilibrium on the undulating floor. It is not easy to catch the real complexion of St Mark's, and these laudable attempts at portraiture are apt to look either lurid or livid. But if you cannot paint the old loose-looking marble slabs, the great panels of basalt and jasper, the crucifixes of which the lonely anguish looks deeper in the vertical light, the tabernacles whose open doors disclose a dark Byzantine image spotted with dull, crooked gems – if you cannot paint these things you can at least grow fond of them. You grow fond even of the old benches of red marble, partly worn away by the breeches of many generations and attached to the base of those wide pilasters of which the precious plating, delightful in its faded brownness, with a faint grey bloom upon it, bulges and yawns a little with honourable age.

IV

Even at first, when the vexatious sense of the city of the Doges reduced to earning its living as a curiosity-shop was in its keenness, there was a great deal of entertainment to be got from lodging on Riva Schiavoni and looking out at the far-shimmering lagoon. There was entertainment indeed in simply getting into the place and observing the queer incidents of a Venetian installation. A great many persons contribute indirectly to this undertaking, and it is surprising how they spring out at you during your novitiate to remind you that they are bound up in some mysterious manner with the constitution of your little establishment. It was an interesting problem for instance

Whistler, San Giorgio, 1879-80

Whistler, Canal. San Canciano, 1879-80

to trace the subtle connection existing between the niece of the landlady and the occupancy of the fourth floor. Superficially it was none too visible, as the young lady in question was a dancer at the Fenice theatre – or when that was closed at the Rossini – and might have been supposed absorbed by her professional duties. It proved necessary, however, that she should hover about the premises in a velvet jacket and a pair of black kid gloves with one little white button; as also, that she should apply a thick coating of powder to her face, which had a charming oval and a sweet weak expression, like that of most of the Venetian maidens, who, as a general thing – it was not a peculiarity of the landlady's niece – are fond of besmearing themselves with flour. You soon recognise that it is not only the many-twinkling lagoon you behold from a habitation on the Riva; you see a little of everything Venetian. Straight across, before my windows, rose the great pink mass of San Giorgio Maggiore, which has for an ugly Palladian church a success beyond all reason. It is a success of position, of colour, of the immense detached *campanile*, tipped with a tall gold angel. I know not whether it is because San Giorgio is so grandly conspicuous, with a great deal of worn, faded-looking brickwork; but for many persons the whole place has a kind of suffusion of rosiness. Asked what may be the leading colour in the Venetian concert, we should inveterately say Pink, and yet without remembering after all that this elegant hue occurs very often. It is a faint, shimmering, airy, watery pink; the bright sea-light seems to flush with it and the pale whitish-green of lagoon and canal to drink it in. There is indeed a great deal of very evident brickwork, which is never fresh or loud in colour, but always burnt out, as it were, always exquisitely mild.

Certain little mental pictures rise before the collector of memories at the simple mention, written or spoken, of the places he has loved. When I hear, when I see, the magical name I have written above these pages, it is not of the great Square that I think, with its strange basilica and its high arcades, nor of the wide mouth of the Grand Canal, with the stately steps and the well-poised dome of the Salute; it is not of the low lagoon, nor the sweet Piazzetta, nor the dark chambers of St Mark's. I simply see a narrow canal in the heart of the city – a patch of green water and a surface of pink wall. The gondola moves slowly; it gives a great smooth swerve, passes under a bridge, and the gondolier's cry, carried over the quiet water, makes a kind of splash in the stillness. A girl crosses the little bridge, which has an arch like a camel's back, with an old shawl on her head, which makes her characteristic and charming; you see her against the sky as you float beneath. The pink of the old wall seems to fill the whole place; it sinks even into the opaque water. Behind the wall is a garden, out of which the long arm of a white June rose – the roses of Venice are splendid – has flung itself by way of spontaneous ornament. On the other side of this small water-way is a great shabby façade of Gothic windows and balconies – balconies on which dirty clothes are hung and under which a cavernous-looking doorway opens from a low flight of slimy water-steps. It is very hot and still, the canal has a queer smell, and the whole place is enchanting.

It is poor work, however, talking about the colour of things in Venice. The fond spectator is perpetually looking at it from his window, when he is not floating about with that delightful sense of being for the moment a part of it, which any gentleman in a gondola is free to entertain. Venetian windows and balconies are a dreadful lure, and while you rest your elbows on these cushioned ledges the precious hours fly away. But in truth Venice isn't in fair weather a place for concentration of mind. The effort required for sitting down to a writing-table is heroic, and the brightest page of MS. looks dull beside the brilliancy of your *milieu*. All nature beckons you forth and murmurs to you sophistically that such hours should be devoted to collecting impressions. Afterwards, in ugly places, at unprivileged times, you can convert your impressions into prose. Fortunately for the present proser the weather wasn't always fine; the first month was wet and windy, and it was better to judge of the matter from an open casement than to respond to the advances of persuasive gondoliers. Even then however there was a constant

Ralph Curtis, The Gondola, 1884

entertainment in the view. It was all cold colour, and the steel-grey floor of the lagoon was stroked the wrong way by the wind. Then there were charming cool intervals, when the churches, the houses, the anchored fishing-boats, the whole gently-curving line of the Riva, seemed to be washed with a pearly white. Later it all turned warm – warm to the eye as well as to other senses. After the middle of May the whole place was in a glow. The sea took on a thousand shades, but they were only infinite variations of blue, and those rosy walls I just spoke of began to flush in the thick sunshine. Every patch of colour, every yard of weather-stained stucco, every glimpse of nestling garden or daub of sky above a *calle*, began to shine and sparkle – began, as the painters say, to "compose". The lagoon was streaked with odd currents, which played across it like huge smooth finger-marks. The gondolas multiplied and spotted it all over; every

gondola and gondolier looking, at a distance, precisely like every other.

There is something strange and fascinating in this mysterious impersonality of the gondola. It has an identity when you are in it, but, thanks to their all being of the same size, shape and colour, and of the same deportment and gait, it has none, or as little as possible, as you see it pass before you. From my windows on the Riva there was always the same silhouette – the long, black, slender skiff, lifting its head and throwing it back a little, moving yet seeming not to move, with the grotesquely-graceful figure on the poop. This figure inclines, as may be, more to the graceful or to the grotesque – standing in the "second position" of the dancing-master, but indulging from the waist upward in a freedom of movement which that functionary would deprecate. One may say as a general thing that there is something rather awkward in the movement even of the most graceful gondolier, and

Sargent, Campo dei Frari, 1880-81

something graceful in the movement of the most awkward. In the graceful men of course the grace predominates, and nothing can be finer than the large, firm way in which, from their point of vantage, they throw themselves over their tremendous oar. It has the boldness of a plunging bird and the regularity of a pendulum. Sometimes, as you see this movement in profile, in a gondola that passes you – see, as you recline on your own low cushions, the arching body of the gondolier lifted up against the sky – it has a kind of nobleness which suggests an image on a Greek frieze. The gondolier at Venice is your very good friend – if you choose him happily –

Whistler, The Traghetto, 1879-80

and on the quality of the personage depends a good deal that of your impressions. He is a part of your daily life, your double, your shadow, your complement. Most people, I think, either like their gondolier or hate him; and if they like him, like him very much. In this case they take an interest in him after his departure; wish him to be sure of employment, speak of him as the gem of gondoliers and tell their friends to be certain to "secure" him. There is usually no difficulty in securing him; there is nothing elusive or reluctant about a gondolier. Nothing would induce me not to believe them for the most part excellent fellows, and the sentimental tourist must always have a kindness for them. More than the rest of the population, of course, they are the children of Venice; they are associated with its idiosyncrasy, with its essence, with its silence, with its melancholy.

When I say they are associated with its silence I should immediately add that they are associated also with its sound. Among themselves they are an extraordinarily talkative company. They chatter at the *traghetti,* where they always have some sharp point under discussion; they bawl across the canals; they bespeak your commands as you approach; they defy each other from afar. If you happen to have a *traghetto* under your window, you are well aware that they are a vocal race. I should go even further than I went just now, and say that the voice of the gondolier is in fact for audibility the dominant or rather the only note of Venice. There is scarcely another heard sound, and that indeed is part of the interest of the place. There is no noise there save distinctly human noise; no rumbling, no vague uproar, nor rattle of wheels and hoofs. It is all articulate and vocal and personal. One may say indeed that Venice is emphatically the city of conversation; people talk all over the place because there is nothing to interfere with its being caught by the ear. Among the populace it is a general family party. The still water carries the voice, and good Venetians exchange confidences at a distance of half a mile. It saves a world of trouble, and they don't like trouble. Their delightful garrulous language helps them to make Venetian life a long *conversazione*. This language, with its soft elisions, its odd transpositions, its kindly contempt for consonants and other disagreeables, has in it something peculiarly human and accommodating. If your gondolier had no other merit he would have the merit that he speaks Venetian. This may rank as a merit even – some people perhaps would say especially – when you don't understand what he says. But he adds to it other graces which make him an agreeable feature in your life. The price he sets on his services is touchingly small, and he has a happy art of being obsequious without being, or at least without seeming, abject. For occasional liberalities he evinces an almost lyrical gratitude. In short he has delightfully good manners, a merit which he shares for the most part with the Venetians at large. One grows very fond of these people, and the reason of one's fondness is the frankness and sweetness of their address. That of the Italian family at large has much to recommend it; but in the Venetian manner there is something peculiarly ingratiating. One feels that the race is old, that it has a long and rich civilisation in its blood, and that if it hasn't been blessed by fortune it has at least been polished by time. It hasn't a genius for stiff morality, and indeed makes few pretensions in that direction. It scruples but scantly to represent the false as the true, and has been accused of cultivating the occasion to grasp and to overreach, and of steering a crooked course – not to your and my advantage – amid the sanctities of property. It has been accused further of loving if not too well at least too often, of being in fine as little austere as possible. I am not sure it is very brave, nor struck with its being very industrious. But it has an unfailing sense of the amenities of life; the poorest Venetian is a natural man of the world.

He is better company than persons of his class are apt to be among the nations of industry and virtue – where people are also sometimes perceived to lie and steal and otherwise misconduct themselves. He has a great desire to please and to be pleased.

V

In that matter at least the cold-blooded stranger begins at last to imitate him; begins to lead a life that shall be before all things easy; unless indeed he allow himself, like Mr Ruskin, to be put out of humour by Titian and Tiepolo. The hours he spends among the pictures are his best hours in Venice, and I am ashamed to have written so much of common things when I might have been making festoons of the names of the masters. Only, when we have covered our page with such festoons what more is left to say? When one has said Carpaccio and Bellini, the Tintoret and the Veronese, one has struck a note that must be left to resound at will. Everything has been said about the mighty painters, and it is of little importance that a pilgrim the more has found them to his taste. "Went this morning to the Academy; was very much pleased with Titian's *Assumption*." That honest phrase has doubtless been written in many a traveller's diary, and was not indiscreet on the part of its author. But it appeals little to the general reader, and we must moreover notoriously not expose our deepest feelings. Since I have mentioned Titian's *Assumption* I must say that there are some people who have been less pleased with it than the observer we have just imagined. It is one of the possible disappointments of Venice, and you may if you like take advantage of your privilege of not caring for it. It imparts a look of great richness to the side of the beautiful room of the Academy on which it hangs; but the same room contains two or three works less known to fame which are equally capable of inspiring a passion. "The *Annunciation* struck me as coarse and superficial": that note was once made in a simple-minded tourist's book. At Venice, strange to say, Titian is altogether a disappointment; the city of his adoption is far from containing the best of him. Madrid, Paris, London, Florence, Dresden, Munich – these are the homes of his greatness.

There are other painters who have but a single home, and the greatest of these is the Tintoret. Close beside him sit Carpaccio and Bellini, who make with him the dazzling Venetian trio. The Veronese may be seen and measured in other places; he is most splendid in Venice, but he shines in Paris and in Dresden. You may walk out of the noon-day dusk of Trafalgar Square in November, and in one of the chambers of the National Gallery see the family of Darius rustling and pleading and weeping at the feet of Alexander. Alexander is a beautiful young Venetian in crimson pantaloons, and the picture sends a glow into the cold London twilight. You may sit before it for an hour and dream you are floating to the water-gate of the Ducal Palace, where a certain old beggar who has one of the handsomest heads in the world – he has sat to a hundred painters for Doges and for personages more sacred – has a prescriptive right to pretend to pull your gondola to the steps and to hold out a greasy immemorial cap. But you must go to Venice in very fact to see the other masters, who form part of your life while you are there, who illuminate your view of the universe. It is difficult to express one's relation to them; the whole Venetian art-world is so near, so familiar, so much an extension and adjunct of the spreading actual, that it seems almost invidious to say one owes more to one of them than to the other. Nowhere, not even in Holland, where the correspondence between the real aspects and the little polished canvases is so constant and so exquisite, do art and life seem so interfused and, as it were, so consanguineous. All the splendour of light and colour, all the Venetian air and the Venetian history are on the walls and ceilings of the palaces; and all the genius of the masters, all the images and visions they have left upon canvas, seem to tremble in the sunbeams and dance upon the waves. That is the perpetual interest of the place – that you live in a certain sort of knowledge as in a rosy cloud. You don't go into the churches and galleries by way of a change from the streets; you go into them

Sargent, Sortie de l'église, 1880-82

because they offer you an exquisite reproduction of the things that surround you. All Venice was both model and painter, and life was so pictorial that art couldn't help becoming so. With all diminutions life is pictorial still, and this fact gives an extraordinary freshness to one's perception of the great Venetian works. You judge of them not as a connoisseur, but as a man of the world, and you enjoy them because they are so social and so true. Perhaps of all works of art that are equally great they demand least reflection on the part of the spectator – they make least of a mystery of being enjoyed. Reflection only confirms your admiration, yet is almost ashamed to show its head. These things speak so frankly and benignantly to the sense that even when they arrive at the highest style – as in the Tintoret's *Presentation of the little Virgin at the Temple* – they are still more familiar.

But it is hard, as I say, to express all this, and it is painful as well to attempt it – painful because in the memory of vanished hours so filled with beauty the consciousness of present loss oppresses. Exquisite hours, enveloped in light and silence, to have known them once is to have always a terrible standard of enjoyment. Certain lovely mornings of May and June come back with an ineffaceable fairness. Venice isn't smothered in flowers at this season, in the manner of Florence and Rome; but the sea and sky themselves seem to blossom and rustle. The gondola waits at the wave-washed steps, and if you are wise you will take your place beside a discriminating companion. Such a companion in Venice should of course be of the sex that discriminates most finely. An intelligent woman who knows her Venice seems doubly intelligent, and it makes no woman's perceptions less keen to be aware that she can't help looking graceful as she is borne over the waves. The handsome Pasquale, with uplifted oar, awaits your command, knowing, in a general way, from observation of your habits, that your intention is to go to see a picture or two. It perhaps doesn't immensely matter what picture you choose: the whole affair is so charming. It is charming to wander through the light and shade of intricate canals, with perpetual architecture above you and perpetual fluidity beneath. It is charming to disembark at the polished steps of a little empty *campo* – a sunny shabby square with an old well in the middle, an old church on one side and tall Venetian windows looking down. Sometimes the windows are

tenantless; sometimes a lady in a faded dressing-gown leans vaguely on the sill. There is always an old man holding out his hat for coppers; there are always three or four small boys dodging possible umbrella-pokes while they precede you, in the manner of custodians, to the door of the church.

VI

The churches of Venice are rich in pictures, and many a masterpiece lurks in the unaccommodating gloom of side-chapels and sacristies. Many a noble work is perched behind the dusty candles and muslin roses of a scantily-visited altar; some of them indeed, hidden behind the altar, suffer in a darkness that can never be explored. The facilities offered you for approaching the picture in such cases are a mockery of your irritated wish. You stand at tip-toe on a three-legged stool, you climb a rickety ladder, you almost mount upon the shoulders of the *custode*. You

Sargent, Campo S. Agnese, 1890

do everything but see the picture. You see just enough to be sure it's beautiful. You catch a glimpse of a divine head, of a fig-tree against a mellow sky, but the rest is impenetrable mystery. You renounce all hope, for instance, of approaching the magnificent Cima da Conegliano in San Giovanni in Bragora; and bethinking yourself of the immaculate purity that shines in the spirit of this master, you renounce it with chagrin and pain. Behind the high altar in that church hangs a *Baptism of Christ* by Cima which I believe has been more or less repainted. You make the thing out in spots, you see it has a fullness of perfection. But you turn away from it with a stiff neck and promise yourself consolation in the Academy and at the Madonna dell' Orto, where two noble works by the same hand – pictures as clear as a summer twilight – present themselves in better circumstances. It may be said as a general thing that you never see the Tintoret. You admire him, you adore him, you think him the greatest of painters, but in the great majority of cases your eyes fail to deal with him. This is partly his own fault; so many of his works have turned to blackness and are positively rotting in their frames. At the Scuola di San Rocco, where there are acres of him, there is scarcely anything at all adequately visible save the immense *Crucifixion* in the upper storey. It is true that in looking at this huge composition you look at many pictures; it has not only a multitude of figures but a wealth of episodes; and you pass from one of these to the other as if you were "doing" a gallery. Surely no single picture in the world contains more of human life; there is everything in it, including the most exquisite beauty. It is one of the greatest things of art; it is always interesting. There are works of the artist which contain touches more exquisite, revelations of beauty more radiant, but there is no other vision of so intense a reality, an execution so splendid. The interest, the impressiveness, of that whole corner of Venice, however melancholy the effect of its gorgeous and ill-lighted chambers, gives a strange importance to a visit to the Scuola. Nothing that all travellers go to see appears to suffer less from the incursions of travellers. It is one of the loneliest booths of the bazaar, and the author of these lines has always had the good fortune, which he wishes to every other traveller, of having it to himself. I think most visitors find the place rather alarming and wicked-looking. They walk about a while among the fitful figures that gleam here and there out of the great tapestry (as it were) with which the painter has hung all the walls, and then, depressed and bewildered by the portentous solemnity of these objects, by strange glimpses of unnatural scenes, by the echo of their lonely footsteps on the vast stone floors, they take a hasty departure, finding themselves again, with a sense of release from

danger, a sense that the *genius loci* was a sort of mad white-washer who worked with a bad mixture, in the bright light of the *campo*, among the beggars, the orange-vendors and the passing gondolas. Solemn indeed is the place, solemn and strangely suggestive, for the simple reason that we shall scarcely find four walls elsewhere that enclose within a like area an equal quantity of genius. The air is thick with it and dense and difficult to breathe; for it was genius that was not happy, inasmuch as it lacked the art to fix itself for ever. It is not immortality that we breathe at the Scuola di San Rocco, but conscious, reluctant mortality.

Fortunately, however, we can turn to the Ducal Palace, where everything is so brilliant and splendid that the poor dusky Tintoret is lifted in spite of himself into the concert. This deeply original building is of course the loveliest thing in Venice, and a morning's stroll there is a wonderful illumination. Cunningly select your hour – half the enjoyment of Venice is a question of dodging – and enter at about one o'clock, when the tourists have flocked off to lunch and the echoes of the charming chambers have gone to sleep among the sunbeams. There is no brighter place in Venice – by which I mean that on the whole there is none half so bright. The reflected sunshine plays up through the great windows from the glittering lagoon and shimmers and twinkles over gilded walls and ceilings. All the history of Venice, all its splendid stately past, glows around you in a strong sea-light. Every one here is magnificent, but the great Veronese is the most magnificent of all. He swims before you in a silver cloud; he thrones in an eternal morning. The deep blue sky burns behind him, streaked across with milky bars; the white colonnades sustain the richest canopies, under which the first gentlemen and ladies in the world both render homage and receive it. Their glorious garments rustle in the air of the sea and their sun-lighted faces are the very complexion of Venice. The mixture of pride and piety, of politics and religion, of art and patriotism, gives a splendid dignity to every scene. Never was a painter more nobly joyous, never did an artist take a greater delight in life, seeing it all as a kind of breezy

Sargent, Interior of the Doges' Palace, 1898

festival and feeling it through the medium of perpetual success. He revels in the gold-framed ovals of the ceilings, multiplies himself there with the fluttering movement of an embroidered banner that tosses itself into the blue. He was the happiest of painters and produced the happiest picture in the world. *The Rape of Europa* surely deserves this title; it is impossible to look at it without aching with envy. Nowhere else in art is such a temperament revealed; never did inclination and opportunity combine to express such enjoyment. The mixture of flowers and gems and brocade, of blooming flesh and shining sea and waving groves, of youth, health, movement, desire – all this is the brightest vision that ever descended upon the soul of a painter. Happy the artist who could entertain such a vision; happy the artist who could paint it as the masterpiece I here recall is painted.

The Tintoret's visions were not so bright as that; but he had several that were radiant enough. In the room that contains the work just cited are several smaller canvases by the greatly more complex genius of the Scuola di San Rocco, which are almost simple in their loveliness, almost happy in their simplicity. They have kept their brightness through the centuries, and they shine with their neighbours in those golden rooms. There is a piece of painting in one of them which is one of the sweetest things in Venice and which reminds one afresh of those wild flowers of execution that bloom so profusely and so unheeded in the dark corners of all of the Tintoret's work. *Pallas chasing away Mars* is, I believe, the name that is given to the picture; and it represents in fact a young woman of noble appearance administering a gentle push to a fine young man in armour, as if to tell him to keep his distance. It is of the gentleness of this push that I speak, the charming way in which she puts out her arm, with a single bracelet on it, and rests her young hand, its rosy fingers parted, on his dark breastplate. She bends her enchanting head with the effort – a head which has all the strange fairness that the Tintoret always sees in women – and the soft, living, flesh-like glow of all these members, over which the brush has scarcely paused in its course, is as pretty an example of genius as all Venice can show.

But why speak of the Tintoret when I can say nothing of the great *Paradise*, which unfolds its somewhat smoky splendour and the wonder of its multitudinous circles in one of the other chambers? If it were not one of the first pictures in the world it would be about the biggest, and we must confess that the spectator gets from it at first chiefly an impression of quantity. Then he sees that this quantity is really wealth; that the dim confusion of faces is a magnificent composition, and that some of the details of this composition are extremely beautiful. It is impossible however in a retrospect of Venice to specify one's happiest hours, though as one looks backward certain ineffaceable moments start here and there into vividness. How is it possible to forget one's visits to the sacristy of the Frari, however frequent they may have been, and the great work of John Bellini which forms the treasure of that apartment?

VII

Nothing in Venice is more perfect than this, and we know of no work of art more complete. The picture is in three compartments: the Virgin sits in the central division with her child; two venerable saints, standing close together, occupy each of the others. It is impossible to imagine anything more finished or more ripe. It is one of those things that sum up the genius of a painter, the experience of a life, the teaching of a school. It seems painted with molten gems, which have only been clarified by time, and it is as solemn as it is gorgeous and as simple as it is deep. Giovanni Bellini is more or less everywhere in Venice, and, wherever he is, almost certain to be first – first, I mean, in his own line: he paints little else than the Madonna and the saints; he has not Carpaccio's care for human life at large, nor the Tintoret's nor that of the Veronese. Some of his greater pictures, however, where several figures are clustered together, have a richness of sanctity that is almost profane. There is one of them on the dark side of the room at the Academy that contains Titian's *Assumption*, which if we could only see it – its position is an inconceivable scandal – would evidently be one of the mightiest of so-called sacred pictures. So too is the Madonna of San Zaccaria, hung in a cold, dim, dreary place, ever so much too high, but so mild and serene, and so grandly disposed and accompanied, that the proper attitude for even the most critical amateur, as he looks at it, strikes one as the bended knee. There is another noble John Bellini, one of the very few in which there is no Virgin, at San Giovanni Crisostomo – a St Jerome, in a red dress, sitting aloft upon the rocks and with a landscape of extraordinary purity behind him. The absence of the peculiarly erect Madonna makes it an interesting surprise among the works of the painter and gives it a somewhat less strenuous air. But it has brilliant beauty and the St Jerome is a delightful old personage.

The same church contains another great picture for which the haunter of these places must find a shrine apart in his memory; one of the most interesting things he will have seen, if not the most brilliant. Nothing appeals more to him than three figures of Venetian ladies which occupy the foreground of a smallish canvas of Sebastian del Piombo, placed above the high altar of San Giovanni Crisostomo. Sebastian was a Venetian by birth, but few of his productions are to be seen in his native place; few indeed are to be seen anywhere. The picture represents the patron-saint of the church, accompanied by other saints and by the worldly votaries I have mentioned. These ladies stand together on the left, holding in their hands little white caskets; two of them are in profile, but the foremost turns her face to the spectator. This face and figure are almost unique among the beautiful things of Venice, and they leave the susceptible observer with the impression of having made, or rather having missed, a strange, a dangerous, but a most valuable, acquaintance. The lady, who is superbly handsome, is the typical Venetian of the sixteenth century, and she remains for the mind the perfect flower of that society. Never was there a greater air of breeding, a deeper expression of tranquil superiority. She walks a goddess – as if she trod without sinking the waves of the Adriatic. It is impossible to conceive a more perfect expression of the aristocratic spirit either in its pride or in its benignity. This magnificent

creature is so strong and secure that she is gentle, and so quiet that in comparison all minor assumptions of calmness suggest only a vulgar alarm. But for all this there are depths of possible disorder in her light-coloured eye.

I had meant however to say nothing about her, for it's not right to speak of Sebastian when one hasn't found room for Carpaccio. These visions come to one, and one can neither hold them nor brush them aside. Memories of Carpaccio, the magnificent, the delightful – it's not for want of such visitations, but only for want of space, that I haven't said of him what I would. There is little enough need of it for Carpaccio's sake, his fame being brighter today – thanks to the generous lamp Mr Ruskin has held up to it – than it has ever been. Yet there is something ridiculous in talking of Venice without making him almost the refrain. He and the Tintoret are the two great realists, and it is hard to say which is the more human, the more various. The Tintoret had the mightier temperament, but Carpaccio, who had the advantage of more newness and more responsibility, sailed nearer to perfection. Here and there he quite touches it, as in the enchanting picture, at the Academy, of St Ursula asleep in her little white bed, in her high clean room, where the angel visits her at dawn; or in the noble St Jerome in his study at S. Giorgio Schiavoni. This latter work is a pearl of sentiment, and I may add without being fantastic a ruby of colour. It unites the most masterly finish with a kind of universal largeness of feeling, and he who has it well in his memory will never hear the name of Carpaccio without a throb of almost personal affection. Such indeed is the feeling that descends upon you in that wonderful little chapel of St George of the Slaves, where this most personal and sociable of artists has expressed all the sweetness of his imagination. The place is small and incommodious, the pictures are out of sight and ill-lighted, the custodian is rapacious, the visitors are mutually intolerable, but the shabby little chapel is a palace of art. Mr Ruskin has written a pamphlet about it which is a real aid to enjoyment, though I can't but think the generous artist, with his keen senses and his just feeling, would have suffered to hear his eulogist declare that one of his other productions – in the Museo Civico of Palazzo Correr, a delightful portrait of two Venetian ladies with pet animals – is the "finest picture in the world". It has no need of that to be thought admirable; and what more can a painter desire?

VIII

May in Venice is better than April, but June is best of all. Then the days are hot, but not too hot, and the nights are more beautiful than the days. Then Venice is rosier than ever in the morning and more golden than ever as the day descends. She seems to expand and evaporate, to multiply all her reflections and iridescences. Then the life of her people and the strangeness of her constitution become a perpetual comedy, or at least a perpetual drama. Then the gondola is your sole habitation, and you spend days between sea and sky. You go to the Lido, though the Lido has been spoiled. When I first saw it, in 1869, it was a very natural place, and there was but a rough lane across the little island from the landing-place to the beach. There was a bathing-place in those days, and a restaurant, which was very bad, but where in the warm evenings your dinner didn't much matter as you sat letting it cool on the wooden terrace that stretched out into the sea. Today the Lido is a part of united Italy and has been made the victim of villainous improvements. A little

Naya studio, Lido landing stage, c.1900

Carlo Naya, Chioggia, c.1890

cockney village has sprung up on its rural bosom and a third-rate boulevard leads from Santa Elisabetta to the Adriatic. There are bitumen walks and gas-lamps, lodging-houses, shops and a *teatro diurno*. The bathing-establishment is bigger than before, and the restaurant as well; but it is a compensation perhaps that the cuisine is no better. Such as it is, however, you won't scorn occasionally to partake of it on the breezy platform under which bathers dart and splash, and which looks out to where the fishing-boats, with sails of orange and crimson, wander along the darkening horizon. The beach at the Lido is still lonely and beautiful, and you can easily walk away from the cockney village. The return to Venice in the sunset is classical and indispensable, and those who at that glowing hour have floated toward the towers that rise out of the lagoon will not easily part with the impression. But you indulge in larger excursions – you go to Burano and Torcello, to Malamocco and Chioggia. Torcello, like the Lido, has been improved; the deeply interesting little cathedral of the eighth century, which stood there on the edge of the sea, as touching in its ruin, with its grassy threshold and its primitive mosaics, as the bleached bones of a human skeleton washed ashore by the tide, has now been restored and made cheerful, and the charm of the place, its strange and suggestive desolation, has well-nigh departed.

It will still serve you as a pretext, however, for a day on the lagoon, especially as you will disembark at Burano

Whistler, The Little Lagoon, 1879-80

and admire the wonderful fisher-folk, whose good looks – and bad manners, I am sorry to say – can scarcely be exaggerated. Burano is celebrated for the beauty of its women and the rapacity of its children, and it is a fact that though some of the ladies are rather bold about it every one of them shows you a handsome face. The children assail you for coppers, and in their desire to be satisfied pursue your gondola into the sea. Chioggia is a larger Burano, and you carry away from either place a half-sad, half-cynical, but altogether pictorial impression; the impression of bright-coloured hovels, of bathing in stagnant canals, of young girls with faces of a delicate shape and a susceptible expression, with splendid heads of hair and complexions smeared with powder, faded yellow shawls that hang like old Greek draperies, and little wooden shoes that click as they go up and down the steps of the convex bridges; of brown-cheeked matrons with lustrous tresses and high tempers, massive throats encased with gold beads, and eyes that meet your own with a certain traditional defiance. The men throughout the islands of Venice are almost as handsome as the women; I have never seen so many good-looking rascals. At Burano and Chioggia they sit mending their nets, or lounge at the street corners, where conversation is always high-pitched, or clamour to you to take a boat; and everywhere they decorate the scene with their splendid colour – cheeks and throats as richly brown as the sails of their fishing-smacks – their sea-faded tatters which are always a "costume", their soft Venetian jargon, and the gallantry with which they wear their hats, an article that nowhere sits so well as on a mass of dense Venetian curls. If you are happy you will find yourself, after a June day in Venice (about ten o'clock), on a balcony that overhangs the Grand Canal, with your elbows on the broad ledge, a cigarette in your teeth and a little good company beside you. The gondolas pass beneath, the watery surface gleams here and there from their lamps, some of which are coloured lanterns that move mysteriously in the darkness. There are some evenings in June when there are too many gondolas, too many lanterns, too many serenades in front of the hotels. The serenading in particular is overdone; but on such a balcony as I speak of you needn't suffer from it, for in the apartment behind you – an accessible refuge – there is more good company, there are more cigarettes. If you are wise you will step back there presently.   *1882*

Whistler, The Isles of Venice, 1879-80

Sargent, Venice, c.1902

THE GRAND CANAL

The honour of representing the plan and the place at their best might perhaps appear, in the City of St Mark, properly to belong to the splendid square which bears the patron's name and which is the centre of Venetian life so far (this is pretty well all the way indeed) as Venetian life is a matter of strolling and chaffering, of gossiping and gaping, of circulating without a purpose, and of staring – too often with a foolish one – through the shop-windows of dealers whose hospitality makes their doorsteps dramatic, at the very vulgarest rubbish in all the modern market. If the Grand Canal, however, is not quite technically a "street", the perverted Piazza is perhaps even less normal; and I hasten to add that I am glad not to find myself studying my subject under the international arcades, or yet (I will go the length of saying) in the solemn presence of the church. For indeed in that case I foresee I should become still more confoundingly conscious of the stumbling-block that inevitably, even with his first few words, crops up in the path of the lover of Venice who rashly addresses himself to expression. "Venetian life" is a mere literary convention, though it be an indispensable figure. The words have played an effective part in the literature of sensibility; they constituted thirty years ago the title of Mr Howells' delightful volume of impressions; but in using them today one owes some frank amends to one's own lucidity. Let me carefully premise therefore that so often as they shall again drop from my pen, so often shall I beg to be regarded as systematically superficial.

Venetian life, in the large old sense, has long since come to an end, and the essential present character of the most melancholy of cities resides simply in its being the most beautiful of tombs. Nowhere else has the past been laid to rest with such tenderness, such a sadness of resignation and remembrance. Nowhere else is the present so alien, so discontinuous, so like a crowd in a cemetery without garlands for the graves. It has no flowers in its hands, but, as a compensation perhaps – and the thing is doubtless more to the point – it has money and little red books. The everlasting shuffle of these irresponsible visitors in the Piazza is contemporary Venetian life. Everything else is only a reverberation of that. The vast mausoleum has a turnstile at the door, and a functionary in a shabby uniform lets you in, as per tariff, to see how dead it is. From this *constatation*, this cold curiosity, proceed all the industry, the prosperity, the vitality of the place. The shopkeepers and gondoliers, the beggars and the models, depend upon it for a living; they are the custodians and the ushers of the great museum – they are even themselves to a certain extent the objects of exhibition. It is in the wide vestibule of the square that the polyglot pilgrims gather most densely; Piazza San Marco is the lobby of the opera in the intervals of the performance. The present fortune of Venice, the lamentable difference, is most easily measured there, and that is why, in the effort to resist our pessimism, we must turn away both from the purchasers and from the vendors of *ricordi*. The *ricordi* that we prefer are gathered best where the gondola glides – best of all on the noble waterway that begins in its glory at the Salute and ends in its abasement at the railway station. It is, however, the cockneyfied Piazzetta (forgive me, shade of St Theodore – has not a brand new café begun to glare there, electrically, this very year?) that introduces us most directly to the great picture by which the Grand Canal works its first spell, and to which a thousand artists, not always with a talent apiece, have

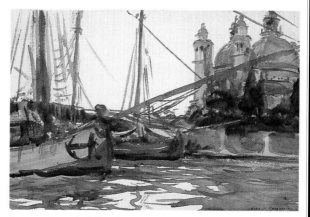

Sargent, S. Maria della Salute, c.1903

Sargent, The Salute, c.1903

paid their tribute. We pass into the Piazzetta to look down the great throat, as it were, of Venice, and the vision must console us for turning our back on St Mark's.

We have been treated to it again and again, of course, even if we have never stirred from home; but that is only a reason the more for catching at any freshness that may be left in the world of photography. It is in Venice above all that we hear the small buzz of this vulgarizing voice of the familiar; yet perhaps it is in Venice too that the picturesque fact has best mastered the pious secret of how to wait for us. Even the classic Salute waits like some great lady on the threshold of her saloon. She is more ample and serene, more seated at her door, than all the copyists have told us, with her domes and scrolls, her scolloped buttresses and statues forming a pompous crown, and her wide steps disposed on the ground like the train of a robe. This fine air of the woman of the world is carried out by the well-bred assurance with which she looks in the direction of her old-fashioned Byzantine neighbour; and the juxtaposition of two churches so distinguished and so different, each splendid in its sort, is a sufficient mark of the scale and range of Venice. However, we ourselves are looking away from St Mark's – we must blind our eyes to that dazzle; without it indeed there are brightnesses and fascinations enough. We see them in abundance even while we look away from the shady steps of the Salute. These steps are cool in the morning, yet I don't know that I can justify my excessive fondness for them any better than I can explain a hundred of the other vague infatuations with which Venice sophisticates the spirit. Under such an influence fortunately one needn't explain – it keeps account of nothing but perceptions and affections. It is from the Salute steps

perhaps, of a summer morning, that this view of the open mouth of the city is most brilliantly amusing. The whole thing composes as if composition were the chief end of human institutions. The charming architectural promontory of the Dogana stretches out the most graceful of arms, balancing in its hand the gilded globe on which revolves the delightful satirical figure of a little weathercock of a woman. This Fortune, this Navigation, or whatever she is called – she surely needs no name – catches the wind in the bit of drapery of which she has divested her rotary bronze loveliness. On the other side of

Sargent, Venice, La Dogana, c.1911

the Canal twinkles and glitters the long row of the happy palaces which are mainly expensive hotels. There is a little of everything everywhere, in the bright Venetian air, but to these houses belongs especially the appearance of sitting, across the water, at the receipt of custom, of watching in their hypocritical loveliness for the stranger and the victim. I call them happy, because even their sordid uses and their vulgar signs melt somehow, with their vague sea-stained pinks and drabs, into that strange gaiety of light and colour which is made up of the reflection of superannuated things. The atmosphere plays over them like a laugh, they are of the essence of the sad old joke. They are almost as charming from other places as they are from their own balconies, and share fully in that universal privilege of Venetian objects which consists of being both the picture and the point of view.

This double character, which is particularly strong in the Grand Canal, adds a difficulty to any control of one's notes. The Grand Canal may be practically, as an impression, the cushioned balcony of a high and well-loved palace – the memory of irresistible evenings, of the sociable elbow, of endless lingering and looking; or it may evoke the restlessness of a fresh curiosity, of methodical inquiry, in a gondola piled with references. There are no references, I ought to mention, in the present remarks, which sacrifice to accident, not to completeness. A rhapsody on Venice is always in order, but I think the catalogues are finished. I should not attempt to write here the names of all the palaces, even if the number of those I find myself able to remember in the immense array were less insignificant. There are many I delight in that I don't know, or at least don't keep, apart. Then there are the bad reasons for preference that are better than the good, and all the sweet bribery of association and recollection. These things, as one stands on the Salute steps, are so many delicate fingers to pick straight out of the row a dear little featureless house which, with its pale green shutters, looks straight across at the great door and through the very keyhole, as it were, of the church, and which I needn't call by a name – a pleasant American name that every one in Venice, these many years, has had on grateful

lips. It is the very friendliest house in all the wide world, and it has, as it deserves to have, the most beautiful position. It is a real *porto di mare,* as the gondoliers say – a port within a port; it sees everything that comes and goes, and takes it all in with practised eyes. Not a tint or a hint of the immense iridescence is lost upon it, and there are days of exquisite colour on which it may fancy itself the heart of the wonderful prism. We wave to it from the Salute steps, which we must decidedly leave if we wish to get on, a grateful hand across the water, and turn into the big white church of Longhena – an empty shaft beneath a perfunctory dome – where an American family and a German party, huddled in a corner upon a pair of benches, are gazing, with a conscientiousness worthy of a better cause, at nothing in particular.

For there is nothing particular in this cold and conventional temple to gaze at save the great Tintoretto of the sacristy, to which we quickly pay our respects, and which we are glad to have for ten minutes to ourselves. The picture, though full of beauty, is not the finest of the master's; but it serves again as well as another to transport – there is no other word – those of his lovers for whom, in far-away days when Venice was an early rapture, this strange and mystifying painter was almost the supreme revelation. The plastic arts may have less to say to us than in the hungry years of youth, and the celebrated picture in general be more of a blank; but more than the others any fine Tintoret still carries us back, calling up not only the rich particular vision but the freshness of the old wonder. Many things come and go, but this great artist remains for us in Venice a part of the company of the mind. The others are there in their obvious glory, but he is the only one for whom the imagination, in our expressive modern phrase, sits up. *The Marriage in Cana*, at the Salute, has all his characteristic and fascinating unexpectedness – the sacrifice of the figure of our Lord, who is reduced to the mere final point of a clever perspective, and the free, joyous presentation of all the other elements of the feast. Why, in spite of this queer one-sidedness, does the picture give us no impression of a lack of what the critics call reverence? For no other reason that I can think of than because it happens to be the work of its author, in whose very mistakes there is a singular wisdom. Mr Ruskin has spoken with sufficient eloquence of the serious loveliness of the row of heads of the women on the right, who talk to each other as they sit at the foreshortened banquet. There could be no better example of the roving independence of the painter's vision, a real spirit of adventure for which his subject was always a cluster of accidents; not an obvious order, but a sort of peopled and agitated chapter of life, in which the figures are submissive pictorial notes. These notes are all there in their beauty and heterogeneity, and if the abundance is of a kind to make the principle of selection seem in comparison timid, yet the sense of "composition" in the spectator – if it happen to exist – reaches out to the painter in peculiar sympathy. Dull must be the spirit of the worker tormented in any field of art with that particular question who is not moved to recognize in the eternal problem the high fellowship of Tintoretto.

If the long reach from this point to the deplorable iron bridge which discharges the pedestrian at the Academy – or, more comprehensively, to the painted and gilded Gothic of the noble Palazzo Foscari – is too much of a curve to be seen at any one point as a whole, it represents the better the arched neck, as it were, of the undulating serpent of which the Canalazzo has the likeness. We pass a dozen historic houses, we note in our passage a hundred component "bits", with the baffled sketcher's sense, and with what would doubtless be, save for our intensely Venetian fatalism, the baffled sketcher's temper. It is the early palaces, of course, and also, to be fair, some of the late, if we could take them one by one, that give the Canal the best of its grand air. The fairest are often cheek-by-jowl with the foulest, and there are few, alas, so fair as to have been completely protected by their beauty. The ages and the generations have worked their will on them, and the wind and the weather have had much to say; but disfigured and dishonoured as they are, with the bruises of their marbles and the patience of their ruin, there is nothing like them in the world, and the long succession of their faded, conscious faces makes of the quiet water-way they overhang a *promenade historique* of which the lesson,

however often we read it, gives, in the depth of its interest, an incomparable dignity to Venice. We read it in the Romanesque arches, crooked today in their very curves, of the early middle-age, in the exquisite individual Gothic of the splendid time, and in the cornices and columns of a decadence almost as proud. These things at present are almost equally touching in their good faith; they have each in their degree so effectually parted with their pride. They have lived on as they could and lasted as they might, and we hold them to no account of their infirmities, for even those of them whose blank eyes today meet criticism with most submission are far less vulgar than the uses we have mainly managed to put them to. We have botched them and patched them and covered them with sordid signs; we have restored and improved them with a merciless taste, and the best of them we have made over to the pedlars. Some of the most striking objects in the finest vistas at present are the huge advertisements of the curiosity-shops.

The antiquity-mongers in Venice have all the courage of their opinion, and it is easy to see how well they know they can confound you with an unanswerable question. What is the whole place but a curiosity-shop, and what are you here for yourself but to pick up odds and ends? "We pick them up *for* you," say these honest Jews, whose prices are marked in dollars, "and who shall blame us if, the flowers being pretty well plucked, we add an artificial rose or two to the composition of the bouquet?" They take care in a word that there be plenty of relics, and their establishments are huge and active. They administer the antidote to pedantry, and you can complain of them only if you never cross their thresholds. If you take this step you are lost, for you have parted with the correctness of your attitude. Venice becomes frankly from such a moment the big depressing dazzling joke in which after all our sense of her contradictions sinks to rest – the grimace of an over-strained philosophy. It's rather a comfort, for the curiosity-shops are amusing. You have bad moments indeed as you stand in their halls of humbug and, in the intervals of haggling, hear through the high windows the soft plash of the sea on the old water-steps, for you think

Sargent, Doorway of a Venetian Palace, c.1905-10

with anger of the noble homes that are laid waste in such scenes, of the delicate lives that must have been, that might still be, led there. You reconstruct the admirable house according to your own needs; leaning on a back balcony, you drop your eyes into one of the little green gardens with which, for the most part, such establishments are exasperatingly blessed, and end by feeling it a shame that you yourself are not in possession. (I take for granted, of course, that as you go and come you are, in imagination, perpetually lodging yourself and setting up your gods; for if this innocent pastime, this borrowing of the mind, be not your favourite sport there is a flaw in the appeal that Venice makes to you.) There may be happy cases in which your envy is tempered, or perhaps I should rather say intensified, by real participation. If you have had the good fortune to enjoy the hospitality of an old Venetian home and to lead your life a little in the painted chambers that still echo with one of the historic names, you have entered by the shortest step into the inner spirit of the place. If it didn't savour of treachery to private kindness I should like to speak frankly of one of these delightful, even though alienated, structures, to refer to it as a splendid example of the old palatial type. But I can only do so in passing, with a hundred precautions, and, lifting the curtain at the edge, drop a commemorative word on the success with which, in this particularly happy instance, the cosmopolite habit, the modern sympathy, the intelligent, flexible attitude, the latest fruit of time, adjust themselves to the great gilded, relinquished shell and try to fill it out. A Venetian palace that has not too grossly suffered and that is not overwhelming by its mass makes almost any life graceful that may be led in it. With cultivated and generous contemporary ways it reveals a pre-established harmony. As you live in it day after day its beauty and its interest sink more deeply into your spirit; it has its moods and its hours and its mystic voices and its shifting expressions. If in the absence of its masters you have happened to have it to yourself for twenty-four hours you will never forget the charm of its haunted stillness, late on the summer afternoon for instance, when the call of playing children comes in behind from the *campo*, nor the way the old ghosts seemed to pass on tip-toe on the marble floors. It gives you practically the essence of the matter that we are considering, for beneath the high balconies Venice comes and goes, and the particular stretch you command contains all the characteristics. Everything has its turn, from the heavy barges of merchandise, pushed by long poles and the patient shoulder, to the floating pavilions of the great serenades, and you may study at your leisure the admirable Venetian arts of managing a boat and organizing a spectacle. Of the beautiful free stroke with which the gondola, especially when there are two oars, is impelled, you never, in the Venetian scene, grow weary; it is always in the picture, and the large profiled action that lets the standing rowers throw themselves forward to a constant recovery has the double value of being, at the fag-end of greatness, the only energetic note. The people from the hotels are always afloat, and, at the hotel pace, the solitary gondolier (like the solitary horseman of the old-fashioned novel) is, I confess, a somewhat melancholy figure. Perched on his poop without a mate, he re-enacts perpetually, in high relief, with his toes turned out, the comedy of his odd and charming movement. He always has a little the look of an absent-minded nursery-maid pushing her small charges in a perambulator.

G.B. Brusa, Regatta Day, Venice, 1891

But why should I risk too free a comparison, where this picturesque and amiable class are concerned? I delight in their sun-burnt complexions and their childish dialect; I know them only by their merits, and I am grossly prejudiced in their favour. They are interesting and touching, and alike in their virtues and their defects human nature is simplified as with a big effective brush. Affecting above all is their dependence on the stranger, the whimsical stranger who swims out of their ken, yet whom Providence sometimes restores. The best of them at any rate are in their line great artists. On the swarming feast-days, on the strange feast-night of the *Redentore*, their steering is a miracle of ease. The master-hands, the celebrities and winners of prizes – you may see them on the private gondolas in spotless white, with brilliant sashes and ribbons, and often with very handsome persons – take the right of way with a pardonable insolence. They penetrate the crush of boats with an authority of their own. The crush of boats, the universal sociable bumping and squeezing, is great when, on the summer nights, the ladies shriek with alarm, the city pays the fiddlers and the illuminated barges, scattering music and song, lead a long train down the Canal. The barges used to be rowed in rhythmic strokes, but now they are towed by the steamer. The coloured lamps, the vocalists before the hotels, are not to my sense the greatest seduction of Venice; but it would be an uncandid sketch of the Canalazzo that shouldn't touch them with indulgence. Taking one nuisance with another, they are probably the prettiest in the world, and if they have in general more magic for the new arrival than for the old Venice-lover, they in any case, at their best, keep up the immemorial tradition. The Venetians have had from the beginning of time the pride of their processions and spectacles, and it's a wonder how with empty pockets they still make a clever show. The Carnival is dead, but these are the scraps of its inheritance. Vauxhall on the water is of course more Vauxhall than ever, with the good fortune of home-made music and of a mirror that reduplicates and multiplies. The feast of the Redeemer – the great popular feast of the year – is a wonderful Venetian Vauxhall. All Venice on this occasion

Sargent, Festa della Regatta, c.1903

takes to the boats for the night and loads them with lamps and provisions. Wedged together in a mass it sups and sings; every boat is a floating arbour, a private *café-concert*. Of all Christian commemorations it is the most ingenuously and harmlessly pagan. Toward morning the passengers repair to the Lido, where, as the sun rises, they plunge, still sociably, into the sea. The night of the *Redentore* has been described, but it would be interesting to have an account, from the domestic point of view, of its usual morrow. It is mainly an affair of the Giudecca, however, which is bridged over from the Zattere to the great church. The pontoons are laid together during the day – it is all done with extraordinary celerity and art – and the bridge is prolonged across the Canalazzo (to Santa Maria Zobenigo), which is my only warrant for glancing at the occasion. We glance at it from our palace windows; lengthening our necks a little, as we look up toward the Salute, we see all Venice, on the July afternoon, so serried as to move slowly, pour across the temporary footway. It is a flock of very good children, and the bridged Canal is their toy. All Venice on such occasions is gentle and friendly; not even all Venice pushes any one into the water.

But from the same high windows we catch without any stretching of the neck a still more indispensable note in the picture, a famous pretender eating the bread of bitterness.

This repast is served in the open air, on a neat little terrace, by attendants in livery, and there is no indiscretion in our seeing that the pretender dines. Ever since the *table d'hôte* in *Candide* Venice has been the refuge of monarchs in want of thrones – she wouldn't know herself without her *rois en exil*. The exile is agreeable and soothing, the gondola lets them down gently. Its movement is an anodyne, its silence a philtre, and little by little it rocks all ambitions to sleep. The proscript has plenty of leisure to write his proclamations and even his memoirs, and I believe he has organs in which they are published; but the only noise he makes in the world is the harmless splash of his oars. He comes and goes along the Canalazzo, and he might be much worse employed. He is but one of the interesting objects it presents, however, and I am by no means sure that he is the most striking. He has a rival, if not in the iron bridge, which, alas, is within our range, at least – to take an immediate example – in the Montecuculi Palace. Far-descended and weary, but beautiful in its crooked old age, with its lovely proportions, its delicate round arches, its carvings and its disks of marble, is the haunted Montecuculi. Those who have a kindness for Venetian gossip like to remember that it was once for a few months the property of Robert Browning, who, however, never lived in it, and who died in the splendid Rezzonico, the residence of his son and a wonderful cosmopolite "document", which, as it presents itself, in an admirable position, but a short way further down the Canal, we can almost see, in spite of the curve, from the window at which we stand. This great seventeenth-century pile, throwing itself upon the water with a peculiar florid assurance, a certain upward toss of its cornice which gives it the air of a rearing sea-horse, decorates immensely – and within, as well as without – the wide angle that it commands.

There is a more formal greatness in the high square Gothic Foscari, just below it, one of the noblest creations of the fifteenth century, a masterpiece of symmetry and majesty. Dedicated today to official uses – it is the property of the State – it looks conscious of the consideration it enjoys, and is one of the few great houses within our range

whose old age strikes us as robust and painless. It is visibly "kept up"; perhaps it is kept up too much; perhaps I am wrong in thinking so well of it. These doubts and fears course rapidly through my mind – I am easily their victim when it is a question of architecture – as they are apt to do today, in Italy, almost anywhere, in the presence of the beautiful, of the desecrated or the neglected. We feel at such moments as if the eye of Mr Ruskin were upon us; we grow nervous and lose our confidence. This makes me inevitably, in talking of Venice, seek a pusillanimous safety in the trivial and the obvious. I am on firm ground in rejoicing in the little garden directly opposite our windows – it is another proof that they really show us everything – and in feeling that the gardens of Venice would deserve a page to themselves. They are infinitely more numerous than the arriving stranger can suppose; they nestle with a charm all their own in the complications of most back-views. Some of them are exquisite, many are large, and even the scrappiest have an artful under-standing, in the interest of colour, with the waterways that edge their foundations. On the small canals, in the hunt for amusement, they are the prettiest surprises of all. The tangle of plants and flowers crowds over the battered walls, the greenness makes an arrangement with the rosy sordid brick. Of all the reflected and liquefied things in Venice, and the number of these is countless, I think the lapping water loves them most. They are numerous on the Canalazzo, but wherever they occur they give a brush to the picture and in particular, it is easy to guess, give a sweetness to the house. Then the elements are complete – the trio of air and water and of things that grow. Venice without them would be too much a matter of the tides and the stones. Even the little trellises of the *traghetti* count charmingly as reminders, amid so much artifice, of the woodland nature of man. The vine-leaves, trained on horizontal poles, make a roof of chequered shade for the gondoliers and ferrymen, who doze there according to opportunity, or chatter or hail the approaching "fare". There is no "hum" in Venice, so that their voices travel far; they enter your windows and mingle even with your dreams. I beg the reader to believe that if I had time to go

Sargent, The Grand Canal, c.1905-10

into everything, I would go into the *traghetti*, which have their manners and their morals, and which used to have their piety. This piety was always a *madonnina*, the protectress of the passage – a quaint figure of the Virgin with the red spark of a lamp at her feet. The lamps appear for the most part to have gone out, and the images doubtless have been sold for *bric-à-brac*. The ferrymen, for aught I know, are converted to Nihilism – a faith consistent happily with a good stroke of business. One of the figures has been left, however – the Madonnetta which gives its name to a *traghetto* near the Rialto. But this sweet survivor is a carven stone inserted ages ago in the corner of an old palace and doubtless difficult of removal. *Pazienza*, the day will come when so marketable a relic will also be extracted from its socket and purchased by the devouring American. I leave that expression, on second thought, standing; but I repent of it when I remember that it is a devouring American – a lady long resident in Venice and whose kindnesses all Venetians, as well as her country-people, know, who has rekindled some of the extinguished tapers, setting up especially the big brave Gothic shrine, of painted and gilded wood, which, on the top of its stout *palo*, sheds its influence on the place of passage opposite the Salute.

If I may not go into those of the palaces this devious discourse has left behind, much less may I enter the great galleries of the Academy, which rears its blank wall, surmounted by the lion of St Mark, well within sight of the windows at which we are still lingering. This wondrous temple of Venetian art – for all it promises little from without – overhangs, in a manner, the Grand Canal, but if we were so much as to cross its threshold we should wander beyond recall. It contains, in some of the most magnificent halls – where the ceilings have all the glory with which the imagination of Venice alone could over-arch a room – some of the noblest pictures in the world; and whether or not we go back to them on any particular occasion for another look, it is always a comfort to know that they are there, as the sense of them on the spot is a part of the furniture of the mind – the sense of them close at hand, behind every wall and under every cover, like the inevitable reverse of a medal, of the side exposed to the air

that reflects, intensifies, completes the scene. In other words, as it was the inevitable destiny of Venice to be painted, and painted with passion, so the wide world of picture becomes, as we live there, and however much we go about our affairs, the constant habitation of our thoughts. The truth is, we are in it so uninterruptedly, at home and abroad, that there is scarcely a pressure upon us to seek it in one place more than in another. Choose your standpoint at random and trust the picture to come to you. This is manifestly why I have not, I find myself conscious, said more about the features of the Canalazzo which occupy the reach between the Salute and the position we have so obstinately taken up. It is still there before us, however, and the delightful little Palazzo Dario, intimately familiar to English and American travellers, picks itself out in the foreshortened brightness. The Dario is covered with the loveliest little marble plates and sculptured circles; it is made up of exquisite pieces – as if there had been only enough to make it small – so that it looks, in its extreme antiquity, a good deal like a house of cards that hold together by a tenure it would be fatal to touch. An old Venetian house dies hard indeed, and I should add that this delicate thing, with submission in every feature, continues to resist the contact of generations of lodgers. It is let out in floors (it used to be let as a whole) and in how many eager hands – for it is in great requisition – under how many fleeting dispensations have we not known and loved it? People are always writing in advance to secure it, as they are to secure the Jenkins's gondolier, and as the gondola passes we see strange faces at the windows – though it's ten to one we recognize them – and the millionth artist coming forth with his traps at the water-gate. The poor little patient Dario is one of the most flourishing booths at the fair.

The faces at the window look out at the great Sansovino – the splendid pile that is now occupied by the Prefect. I feel decidedly that I don't object as I ought to the palaces of the sixteenth and seventeenth centuries. Their pretensions impose upon me, and the imagination peoples them more freely than it can people the interiors of the prime. Was not moreover this masterpiece of Sansovino once occupied by the Venetian post-office, and thereby intimately connected with an ineffaceable first impression of the author of these remarks? He had arrived, wondering, palpitating, twenty-three years ago, after nightfall, and, the first thing on the morrow, had repaired to the post-office for his letters. They had been waiting a long time and were full of delayed interest, and he returned with them to the gondola and floated slowly down the Canal. The mixture, the rapture, the wonderful temple of the *poste restante*, the beautiful strangeness, all humanized by good news – the memory of this abides with him still, so that there always proceeds from the splendid water-front I speak of a certain secret appeal, something that seems to have been uttered first in the sonorous chambers of youth. Of course this association falls to the ground – or rather splashes into the water – if I am the victim of a confusion. *Was* the edifice in question twenty-three years ago the post-office, which has occupied since, for many a day, very much humbler quarters? I am afraid to take the proper steps for finding out, lest I should learn that during these years I have misdirected my emotion. A better reason for the sentiment, at any rate, is that such a great house has surely, in the high beauty of its tiers, a refinement of its own. They make one think of colosseums and aqueducts and bridges, and they constitute doubtless, in Venice, the most pardonable specimen of the imitative. I have even a timid kindness for the huge Pesaro, far down the Canal, whose main reproach, more even than the coarseness of its forms, is its swaggering size, its want of consideration for the general picture, which the early examples so reverently respect. The Pesaro is as far out of the frame as a modern hotel, and the Cornaro, close to it, oversteps almost equally the modesty of art. One more thing they and their kindred do, I must add, for which, unfortunately, we can patronize them less. They make even the most elaborate material civilization of the present day seem woefully shrunken and bourgeois, for they simply – I allude to the biggest palaces – can't be lived in as they were intended to be. The modern tenant may take in all the magazines, but he bends not the bow of Achilles. He occupies the place, but he doesn't fill it, and he has

guests from the neighbouring inns with ulsters and Baedekers. We are far at the Pesaro, by the way, from our attaching window, and we take advantage of it to go in rather a melancholy mood to the end. The long straight vista from the Foscari to the Rialto, the great middle stretch of the Canal, contains, as the phrase is, a hundred objects of interest, but it contains most the bright oddity of its general Deluge air. In all these centuries it has never got over its resemblance to a flooded city; for some reason or other it is the only part of Venice in which the houses look as if the waters had overtaken them. Everywhere else they reckon with them – have chosen them; here alone the lapping seaway seems to confess itself an accident.

There are persons who hold this long, gay, shabby, spotty perspective, in which, with its immense field of confused reflection, the houses have infinite variety, the dullest expanse in Venice. It was not dull, we imagine, for Lord Byron, who lived in the midmost of the three Mocenigo palaces, where the writing-table is still shown at which he gave the rein to his passions. For other observers it is sufficiently enlivened by so delightful a creation as the Palazzo Loredan, once a masterpiece and at present the Municipio, not to speak of a variety of other immemorial bits whose beauty still has a degree of freshness. Some of the most touching relics of early Venice are here – for it was here she precariously clustered – peeping out of a submersion more pitiless than the sea. As we approach the Rialto indeed the picture falls off and a comparative commonness suffuses it. There is a wide paved walk on either side of the Canal, on which the waterman – and who in Venice is not a waterman? – is prone to seek repose. I speak of the summer days – it is the summer Venice that is the visible Venice. The big tarry barges are drawn up at the *fondamenta*, and the bare-legged boatmen, in faded blue cotton, lie asleep on the hot stones. If there were no colour anywhere else there would be enough in their tanned personalities. Half the low doorways open into the warm interior of waterside drinking-shops, and here and there, on the quay, beneath the bush that overhangs the door, there are rickety tables and chairs. Where in Venice is there not the amusement of

Sargent, Gondoliers' Siesta, c. 1905

character and of detail? The tone in this part is very vivid, and is largely that of the brown plebeian faces looking out of the patchy miscellaneous houses – the faces of fat undressed women and of other simple folk who are not aware that they enjoy, from balconies once doubtless patrician, a view the knowing ones of the earth come thousands of miles to envy them. The effect is enhanced by the tattered clothes hung to dry in the windows, by the sun-faded rags that flutter from the polished balustrades – these are ivory-smooth with time; and the whole scene profits by the general law that renders decadence and ruin in Venice more brilliant than any prosperity. Decay is in this extraordinary place golden in tint and misery *couleur de rose*. The gondolas of the correct people are unmitigated sable, but the poor market-boats from the islands are kaleidoscopic.

The Bridge of the Rialto is a name to conjure with, but, honestly speaking, it is scarcely the gem of the composition. There are of course two ways of taking it – from the water or from the upper passage, where its small shops and booths abound in Venetian character; but it mainly counts as a feature of the Canal when seen from the gondola or even from the awful *vaporetto*. The great curve of its single arch is much to be commended, especially when, coming from the direction of the railway-station, you see it frame with its sharp compass-line the perfect picture, the reach of the Canal on the other side. But the backs of the little shops make from the water a graceless collective hump, and the inside view is the diverting one. The big arch of the bridge – like the arches of all the bridges – is the waterman's friend in wet weather. The gondolas, when it rains, huddle beside the peopled barges, and the young ladies from the hotels, vaguely fidgeting, complain of the communication of insect life. Here indeed is a little of everything, and the jewellers of this celebrated precinct – they have their immemorial row – make almost as fine a show as the fruiterers. It is a universal market, and a fine place to study Venetian types. The produce of the islands is discharged there, and the fishmongers announce their presence. All one's senses indeed are vigorously attacked; the whole place is violently hot and bright, all odorous and noisy.

The churning of the screw of the *vaporetto* mingles with the other sounds – not indeed that this offensive note is confined to one part of the Canal. But just here the little piers of the resented steamer are particularly near together, and it seems somehow to be always kicking up the water. As we go further down we see it stopping exactly beneath the glorious windows of the Ca' d' Oro. It has chosen its position well, and who shall gainsay it for having put itself under the protection of the most romantic façade in Europe? The companionship of these objects is a symbol; it expresses supremely the present and the future of Venice. Perfect, in its prime, was the marble Ca' d' Oro, with the noble recesses of its *loggie*, but even then it probably never "met a want", like the successful *vaporetto*. If, however, we are not to go into the Museo Civico – the old Museo Correr, which rears a staring renovated front far down on the left, near the station, so also we must keep out of the great vexed question of steam on the Canalazzo, just as a while since we prudently kept out of the Accademia. These are expensive and complicated excursions. It is obvious that if the *vaporetti* have contributed to the ruin of the gondoliers, already hard pressed by fate, and to that of the palaces, whose foundations their waves undermine, and that if they have robbed the Grand Canal of the supreme distinction of its tranquillity, so on the other hand they have placed " rapid transit", in the New York phrase, in everybody's reach, and enabled everybody – save indeed those who wouldn't for the world – to rush about Venice as furiously as people rush about New York. The suitability of this consummation needn't be pointed out.

Even we ourselves, in the irresistible contagion, are going so fast now that we have only time to note in how clever and costly a fashion the Museo Civico, the old Fondaco dei Turchi, has been reconstructed and restored. It is a glare of white marble without, and a series of showy majestic halls within, where a thousand curious mementos and relics of old Venice are gathered and classified. Of its miscellaneous treasures I fear I may perhaps frivolously prefer the series of its remarkable living Longhis, an illustration of manners more copious than the celebrated

Sargent, Venetian Doorway, c.1900

Carpaccio, the two ladies with their little animals and their long sticks. Wonderful indeed today are the museums of Italy, where the renovations and the *belle ordonnance* speak of funds apparently unlimited, in spite of the fact that the numerous custodians frankly look starved. What is the pecuniary source of all this civic magnificence – it is shown in a hundred other ways – and how do the Italian cities manage to acquit themselves of expenses that would be formidable to communities richer and doubtless less aesthetic? Who pays the bills for the expressive statues alone, the general exuberance of sculpture, with which every *piazzetta* of almost every village is patriotically decorated? Let us not seek an answer to the puzzling question, but observe instead that we are passing the mouth of the populous Canareggio, next widest of the water-ways, where the race of Shylock abides, and at the corner of which the big colourless church of San Geremia stands gracefully enough on guard. The Canareggio, with its wide lateral footways and humpbacked bridges, makes on the feast of St John an admirable noisy, tawdry theatre for one of the prettiest and the most infantile of the Venetian processions.

The rest of the course is a reduced magnificence, in spite of interesting bits, of the battered pomp of the Pesaro and the Cornaro, of the recurrent memories of royalty in exile which cluster about the Palazzo Vendramin Calergi, once the residence of the Comte de Chambord and still that of his half-brother, in spite too of the big Papadopoli gardens, opposite the station, the largest private grounds in Venice, but of which Venice in general mainly gets the benefit in the usual form of irrepressible greenery climbing over walls and nodding at water. The rococo church of the

Sargent, Palazzo Labia with the Campanile of San Geremia, c.1906

Scalzi is here, all marble and malachite, all a cold, hard glitter and a costly, curly ugliness, and here too, opposite, on the top of its high steps, is San Simeone Profeta, I won't say immortalized, but unblushingly misrepresented, by the perfidious Canaletto. I shall not stay to unravel the mystery of this prosaic painter's malpractices; he falsified without fancy, and as he apparently transposed at will the objects he reproduced, one is never sure of the particular view that may have constituted his subject. It would look exactly like such and such a place if almost everything were not different. San Simeone Profeta appears to hang there upon the wall; but it is on the wrong side of the Canal and the other elements quite fail to correspond. One's confusion is the greater because one doesn't know that everything may not really have changed, even beyond all probability – though it's only in America that churches cross the street or the river – and the mixture of the recognizable and the different makes the ambiguity maddening, all the more that the painter is almost as attaching as he is bad. Thanks at any rate to the white church, domed and porticoed, on the top of its steps, the traveller emerging for the first time upon the terrace of the railway-station seems to have a Canaletto before him. He speedily discovers indeed even in the presence of this scene of the final accents of the Canalazzo – there is a charm in the old pink warehouses on the hot *fondamenta* – that he has something much better. He looks up and down at the gathered gondolas; he has his surprise after all, his little first Venetian thrill; and as the terrace of the station ushers in these things we shall say no harm of it, though it is not lovely. It is the beginning of his experience, but it is the end of the Grand Canal.   *1892*

TWO OLD HOUSES AND THREE YOUNG WOMEN

There are times and places that come back yet again, but that, when the brooding tourist puts out his hand to them, meet it a little slowly, or even seem to recede a step, as if in slight fear of some liberty he may take. Surely they should know by this time that he is capable of taking none. He has his own way – he makes it all right. It now becomes just a part of the charming solicitation that it presents precisely a problem – that of *giving* the particular thing as much as possible without at the same time giving it, as we say, away. There are considerations, proprieties, a necessary indirectness – he must use, in short, a little art. No necessity, however, more than this, makes him warm to his work, and thus it is that, after all, he hangs his three pictures.

I

The evening that was to give me the first of them was by no means the first occasion of my asking myself if that inveterate "style" of which we talk so much be absolutely conditioned – in dear old Venice and elsewhere – on decrepitude. Is it the style that has brought about the decrepitude, or the decrepitude that has, as it were, intensified and consecrated the style? There is an ambiguity about it all that constantly haunts and beguiles. Dear old Venice has lost her complexion, her figure, her reputation, her self-respect; and yet, with it all, has so puzzlingly not lost a shred of her distinction. Perhaps indeed the case is simpler than it seems, for the poetry of misfortune is familiar to us all, whereas, in spite of a stroke here and there of some happy justice that charms, we scarce find ourselves anywhere arrested by the poetry of a run of luck. The misfortune of Venice being, accordingly, at every point, what we most touch, feel and see, we end by assuming it to be of the essence of her dignity; a consequence, we become aware, by the way, sufficiently

discouraging to the general application or pretension of style, and all the more that, to make the final felicity deep, the original greatness must have been something tremendous. If it be the ruins that are noble we have known plenty that were not, and moreover there are degrees and varieties: certain monuments, solid survivals, hold up their heads and decline to ask for a grain of your pity. Well, one knows of course when to keep one's pity to oneself; yet one clings, even in the face of the colder stare, to one's prized Venetian privilege of making the sense of doom and decay a part of every impression. Cheerful work, it may be said of course; and it is doubtless only in Venice that you gain more by such a trick than you lose. What was most beautiful is gone; what was next most beautiful is, thank goodness, going – that, I think, is the monstrous description of the better part of your thought. Is it really your fault if the place makes you want so desperately to read history into everything?

You do that wherever you turn and wherever you look, and you do it, I should say, most of all at night. It comes to you there with longer knowledge, and with all deference to what flushes and shimmers, that the night is the real time. It perhaps even wouldn't take much to make you award the palm to the nights of winter. This is certainly true for the form of progression that is most characteristic, for every question of departure and arrival by gondola. The little closed cabin of this perfect vehicle, the movement, the darkness and the plash, the indistinguishable swerves and twists, all the things you don't see and all the things you do feel – each dim recognition and obscure arrest is a possible throb of your sense of being floated to your doom, even when the truth is simply and sociably that you are going out to tea. Nowhere else is anything as innocent so mysterious, nor anything as mysterious so pleasantly deterrent to protest. These are the moments when you are most daringly Venetian, most content to leave cheap trippers and other aliens the high light of the mid-lagoon and the pursuit of pink and gold. The splendid day is good enough for *them*; what is best for you is to stop at last, as you are now stopping, among clustered *pali* and softly-shifting poops and prows, at a great flight of water-steps that play their admirable part in the general effect of a great entrance. The high doors stand open from them to the paved chamber of a basement tremendously tall and not vulgarly lighted, from which, in turn, mounts the slow stone staircase that draws you further on. The great point is, that if you are worthy of this impression at all, there isn't a single item of it of which the association isn't noble. Hold to it fast that there is no other such dignity of arrival as arrival by water. Hold to it that to float and slacken and gently bump, to creep out of the low, dark *felze* and make the few guided movements and find the strong crooked and offered arm, and then, beneath lighted palace-windows, pass up the few damp steps on the precautionary carpet – hold to it that these things constitute a preparation of which the only defect is that it may sometimes perhaps really prepare too much. It's so stately that what can come after? – it's so good in itself that what, upstairs, as we comparative vulgarians say, can be better? Hold to it, at any rate, that if a lady, in especial, scrambles out of a carriage, tumbles out of a cab, flops out of a tram-car, and hurtles, projectile-like, out of a "lightning-elevator", she alights from the Venetian conveyance as Cleopatra may have stepped from her barge. Upstairs – whatever may be yet in store for her – her entrance shall still advantageously enjoy the support most opposed to the "momentum" acquired. The beauty of the matter has been in the absence of all momentum – elsewhere so scientifically applied to us, from behind, by the terrible life of our day – and in the fact that, as the elements of slowness, the felicities of deliberation, doubtless thus all hang together, the last of calculable dangers is to enter a great Venetian room with a rush.

Not the least happy note, therefore, of the picture I am trying to frame is that there was absolutely no rushing; not only in the sense of a scramble over marble floors, but, by reason of something dissuasive and distributive in the very air of the place, a suggestion, under the fine old ceilings and among types of face and figure abounding in the unexpected, that here were many things

to consider. Perhaps the simplest rendering of a scene into the depths of which there are good grounds of discretion for not sinking would be just this emphasis on the value of the unexpected for such occasions – with due qualification, naturally, of its degree. Unexpectedness pure and simple, it is needless to say, may easily endanger any social gathering, and I hasten to add moreover that the figures and faces I speak of were probably not in the least unexpected to each other. The stage they occupied was a stage of variety – Venice has ever been a garden of strange social flowers. It is only as reflected in the consciousness of the visitor from afar – brooding tourist even call him, or sharp-eyed bird on the branch – that I attempt to give you the little drama; beginning with the felicity that most appealed to him, the visible, unmistakable fact that he was the only representative of his class. The whole of the rest of the business was but what he saw and felt and fancied – what he was to remember and what he was to forget. Through it all, I may say distinctly, he clung to his great Venetian clue – the explanation of everything by the historic idea. It was a high historic house, with such a quantity of recorded past twinkling in the multitudinous candles that one grasped at the idea of something waning and displaced, and might even fondly and secretly nurse the conceit that what one was having was just the very last. Wasn't it certainly, for instance, no mere illusion that there is no appreciable future left for such manners – an urbanity so comprehensive, a form so transmitted, as those of such a hostess and such a host? The future is for a different conception of the graceful altogether – so far as it's for a conception of the graceful at all. Into that computation I shall not attempt to enter; but these representative products of an antique culture, at least, and one of which the secret seems more likely than not to be lost, were not common, nor indeed was any one else – in the circle to which the picture most insisted on restricting itself.

Neither, on the other hand, was any one either very beautiful or very fresh: which was again, exactly, a precious "value" on an occasion that was to shine most, to the imagination, by the complexity of its references.

Such old, old women with such old, old jewels; such ugly, ugly ones with such handsome, becoming names; such battered, fatigued gentlemen with such inscrutable decorations; such an absence of youth, for the most part, in either sex – of the pink and white, the "bud" of new worlds; such a general personal air, in fine, of being the worse for a good deal of wear in various old ones. It was not a society – that was clear – in which little girls and boys set the tune; and there was that about it all that might well have cast a shadow on the path of even the most successful little girl. Yet also – let me not be rudely inexact – it was in honour of youth and freshness that we had all been convened. The *fiançailles* of the last – unless it were the last but one – unmarried daughter of the house had just been brought to a proper climax; the contract had been signed, the betrothal rounded off – I'm not sure that the civil marriage hadn't, that day, taken place. The occasion then had in fact the most charming of heroines and the most ingenuous of heroes, a young man, the latter, all happily suffused with a fair Austrian blush. The young lady had had, besides other more or less shining recent ancestors, a very famous paternal grandmother, who had played a great part in the political history of her time and whose portrait, in the taste and dress of 1830, was conspicuous in one of the rooms. The granddaughter of this celebrity, of royal race, was strikingly like her and, by a fortunate stroke, had been habited, combed, curled in a manner exactly to reproduce the portrait. These things were charming and amusing, as indeed were several other things besides. The great Venetian beauty of our period was there, and nature had equipped the great Venetian beauty for her part with the properest sense of the suitable, or in any case with a splendid generosity – since on the ideally suitable *character* of so brave a human symbol who shall have the last word? This responsible agent was at all events the beauty in the world about whom probably, most, the absence of question (an absence never wholly propitious) would a little smugly and monotonously flourish: the one thing wanting to the interest she inspired was thus the possibility of ever discussing it. There were plenty of suggestive subjects round about, on the other hand, as to which the exchange of ideas would by no means necessarily have dropped. You profit to the full at such times by all the old voices, echoes, images – by that element of the history of Venice which represents all Europe as having at one time and another revelled or rested, asked for pleasure or for patience there; which gives you the place supremely as the refuge of endless strange secrets, broken fortunes and wounded hearts.

II

There had been, on lines of further or different speculation, a young Englishman to luncheon, and the young Englishman had proved "sympathetic"; so that when it was a question afterwards of some of the more hidden treasures, the browner depths of the old churches, the case became one for mutual guidance and gratitude – for a small afternoon tour and the wait of a pair of friends in the warm little *campi*, at locked doors for which the nearest urchin had scurried off to fetch the keeper of the key. There are few brown depths today into which the light of the hotels doesn't shine, and few hidden treasures about which pages enough, doubtless, haven't already been printed: my business, accordingly, let me hasten to say, is not now with the fond renewal of any discovery – at least in the order of impressions most usual. Your discovery may be, for that matter, renewed every week; the only essential is the good luck – which a fair amount of practice has taught you to count upon – of not finding, for the particular occasion, other discoverers in the field. Then, in the quiet corner, with the closed door – then in the presence of the picture and of your companion's sensible emotion – not only the original happy moment, but everything else, is renewed. Yet once again it can all come back. The old custode, shuffling about in the dimness, jerks away, to make sure of his tip, the old curtain that isn't much more modern than the wonderful work itself. He does his best to create light where light can never be; but you have your practised groping gaze, and in guiding the young eyes of your less confident

Sargent, San Giuseppe di Castello, c.1903-4

associate, moreover, you feel you possess the treasure. These are the most refined pleasures that Venice has still to give, these odd happy passages of communication and response.

But the point of my reminiscence is that there were other communications that day, as there were certainly other responses. I have forgotten exactly what it was we were looking for – without much success – when we met the three Sisters. Nothing requires more care, as a long knowledge of Venice works in, than not to lose the useful faculty of getting lost. I had so successfully done my best to preserve it that I could at that moment conscientiously profess an absence of any suspicion of where we might be. It proved enough that, wherever we were, we were where the three sisters found us. This was on a little bridge near a big *campo*, and a part of the charm of the matter was the theory that it was very much out of the way. They took us promptly in hand – they were only walking over to San Marco to match some coloured wool for the manufacture of such belated cushions as still bloom with purple and green in the long leisures of old palaces; and that mild errand could easily open a parenthesis. The obscure church we had feebly imagined we were looking for proved, if I am not mistaken, that of the sisters' parish; as to which I have but a confused recollection of a large grey void and of admiring for the first time a fine work of art of which I have now quite lost the identity. This was the effect of the charming beneficence of the three sisters, who presently were to give our adventure a turn in the emotion of which everything that had preceded seemed as nothing. It actually strikes me even as a little dim to have been told by them, as we all fared together, that a certain low, wide house, in a small square as to which I found myself without particular association, had been in the far-off time the residence of George Sand. And yet this was a fact that, though I could then only feel it must be for another day, would in a different connection have set me richly reconstructing.

Madame Sand's famous Venetian year has been of late immensely in the air – a tub of soiled linen which the muse of history, rolling her sleeves well up, has not even yet quite ceased energetically and publicly to wash. The house in question must have been the house to which the wonderful lady betook herself when, in 1834, after the dramatic exit of Alfred de Musset, she enjoyed that remarkable period of rest and refreshment with the so long silent, the but recently rediscovered, reported, extinguished, Doctor Pagello. As an old Sandist – not exactly indeed of the *première heure*, but of the fine high noon and golden afternoon of the great career – I had been, though I confess too inactively, curious as to a few points in the topography of the eminent adventure to which I here allude; but had never got beyond the little public fact, in itself always a bit of a thrill to the Sandist, that the present Hotel Danieli had been the scene of its first remarkable stages. I am not sure indeed that the curiosity I speak of has not at last, in my breast, yielded to another form of wonderment – truly to the rather rueful question of why we have so continued to concern ourselves, and why the fond observer of the footprints of genius is likely so to continue, attentive to an altercation neither in itself and in its day, nor in its preserved and attested records, at all positively edifying. The answer to such an inquiry would doubtless reward patience, but I fear we can now glance at its possibilities only long enough to say that interesting persons – so they be of a

Sargent, Ponte della Canonica, c.1903-4

sufficiently approved and established interest – render in some degree interesting whatever happens to them, and give it an importance even when very little else (as in the case I refer to) may have operated to give it a dignity. Which is where I leave the issue of further identifications.

For the three sisters, in the kindest way in the world, had asked us if we already knew their sequestered home and whether, in case we didn't, we should be at all amused to see it. My own acquaintance with them, though not of recent origin, had hitherto lacked this enhancement, at which we both now grasped with the full instinct, indescribable enough, of what it was likely to give. But how, for that matter, either, can I find the right expression of what was to remain with us of this episode? It is the fault of the sad-eyed old witch of Venice that she so easily puts more into things that can pass under the common names that do for them elsewhere. Too much for a rough sketch was to be seen and felt in the home of the three sisters, and in the delightful and slightly pathetic deviation of their doing us so simply and freely the honours of it. What was most immediately marked was their resigned cosmopolite state, the effacement of old conventional lines by foreign contact and example; by the action, too, of causes full of a special interest, but not to be emphasised perhaps – granted indeed they be named at all – without a certain sadness of sympathy. If "style", in Venice, sits among ruins, let us always lighten our tread when we pay her a visit.

Our steps were in fact, I am happy to think, almost soft enough for a death-chamber as we stood in the big, vague *sala* of the three sisters, spectators of their simplified state and their beautiful blighted rooms, the memories, the portraits, the shrunken relics of nine Doges. If I wanted a first chapter it was here made to my hand; the painter of life and manners, as he glanced about, could only sigh – as he so frequently has to – over the vision of so much more truth than he can use. What on earth is the need to "invent", in the midst of tragedy and comedy that never cease? Why, with the subject itself, all round, so inimitable, condemn the picture to the silliness of trying not to be aware of it? The charming lonely girls, carrying so simply

their great name and fallen fortunes, the despoiled *decaduta* house, the unfailing Italian grace, the space so out of scale with actual needs, the absence of books, the presence of ennui, the sense of the length of the hours and the shortness of everything else – all this was a matter not only for a second chapter and a third, but for a whole volume, a *dénouement* and a sequel.

This time, unmistakably, it *was* the last – Wordsworth's stately "shade of that which once was great"; and it was almost as if our distinguished young friends had consented to pass away slowly in order to treat us to the vision. Ends are only ends in truth, for the painter of pictures, when they are more or less conscious and prolonged. One of the sisters had been to London, whence she had brought back the impression of having seen at the British Museum a room exclusively filled with books and documents devoted to the commemoration of her family. She must also then have encountered at the National Gallery the exquisite specimen of an early Venetian master in which one of her ancestors, then head of the State, kneels with so sweet a dignity before the Virgin and Child. She was perhaps old enough, none the less, to have seen this precious work taken down from the wall of the room in which we sat and – on terms so far too easy – carried away for ever; and not too young, at all events, to have been present, now and then, when her candid elders, enlightened too late as to what their sacrifice might really have done for them, looked at each other with the pale hush of the irreparable. We let ourselves note that these were matters to put a great deal of old, old history into sweet young Venetian faces.

III

In Italy, if we come to that, this particular appearance is far from being only in the streets, where we are apt most to observe it – in countenances caught as we pass and in the objects marked by the guide-books with their respective stellar allowances. It is behind the walls of the houses that old, old history is thick and that the multiplied stars of Baedeker might often best find their application. The feast of St John the Baptist is the feast of the year in Florence, and it seemed to me on that night that I could have scattered about me a handful of these signs. I had the pleasure of spending a couple of hours on a signal high terrace that overlooks the Arno, as well as in the galleries that open out to it, where I met more than ever the pleasant curious question of the disparity between the old conditions and the new manners. Make our manners, we moderns, as good as we can, there is still no getting over it that they are not good enough for many of the great places. This was one of those scenes, and its greatness came out to the full into the hot Florentine evening, in which the pink and golden fires of the pyrotechnics arranged on Ponte Carraja – the occasion of our assembly – lighted up the large issue. The "good people" beneath were a huge, hot, gentle, happy family; the fireworks on the bridge, kindling river as well as sky, were delicate and charming; the terrace connected the

Sargent, Rio di San Salvatore, c.1903-4

two wings that give bravery to the front of the palace, and the close-hung pictures in the rooms, open in a long series, offered to a lover of quiet perambulation an alternative hard to resist.

Wherever he stood – on the broad loggia, in the cluster of company, among bland ejaculations and liquefied ices, or in the presence of the mixed masters that led him from wall to wall – such a seeker for the spirit of each occasion could only turn it over that in the first place this was an intenser, finer little Florence than ever, and that in the second the testimony was again wonderful to former fashions and ideas. What did they do, in the other time, the time of so much smaller a society, smaller and fewer fortunes, more taste perhaps as to some particulars, but fewer tastes, at any rate, and fewer habits and wants – what did they do with chambers so multitudinous and so vast? Put their "state" at its highest – and we know of many ways in which it must have broken down – how did they live in them without the aid of variety? How did they, in minor communities in which every one knew every one, and every one's impression and effect had been long, as we say, discounted, find representation and emulation sufficiently amusing? Much of the charm of thinking of it, however, is doubtless that we are not able to say. This leaves us with the conviction that does them most honour: the old generations built and arranged greatly for the simple reason that they liked it, and they could bore themselves – to say nothing of each other, when it came to that – better in noble conditions than in mean ones.

It was not, I must add, of the far-away Florentine age that I most thought, but of periods more recent and of which the sound and beautiful house more directly spoke. If one had always been homesick for the Arno-side of the seventeenth and eighteenth centuries, here was a chance, and a better one than ever, to taste again of the cup. Many of the pictures – there was a charming quarter of an hour when I had them to myself – were bad enough to have passed for good in those delightful years. Shades of Grand-Dukes encompassed me – Dukes of the pleasant later sort who weren't really grand. There was still the sense of having come too late – yet not too late, after all, for this glimpse and this dream. My business was to people the place – its own business had never been to save us the trouble of understanding it. And then the deepest spell of all was perhaps that just here I was supremely out of the way of the so terribly actual Florentine question. This, as all the world knows, is a battle-ground, today, in many journals, with all Italy practically pulling on one side and all England, America and Germany pulling on the other: I speak of course of the more or less articulate opinion. The "improvement," the rectification of Florence is in the air, and the problem of the particular ways in which, given such desperately delicate cases, these matters should be understood. The little treasure-city is, if there ever was one, a delicate case – more delicate perhaps than any other in the world save that of our taking on ourselves to persuade the Italians that they mayn't do as they like with their own. They so absolutely may that I profess I see no happy issue from the fight. It will take more tact than our combined tactful genius may at all probably muster to convince them that their own is, by an ingenious logic, much rather *ours*. It will take more subtlety still to muster for them that truly dazzling show of examples from which they may learn that what in general is "ours" shall appear to them as a rule a sacrifice to beauty and a triumph of taste. The situation, to the truly analytic mind, offers in short, to perfection, all the elements of despair; and I am afraid that if I hung back, at the Corsini palace, to woo illusions and invoke the irrelevant, it was because I could think, in the conditions, of no better way to meet the acute responsibility of the critic than just to shirk it.

1899

CASA ALVISI

Invited to "introduce" certain pages of cordial and faithful reminiscence from another hand[†], in which a frankly predominant presence seems to live again, I undertook that office with an interest inevitably somewhat sad – so passed and gone today is so much of the life suggested. Those who fortunately knew Mrs Bronson will read into her notes still more of it – more of her subject, more of herself too, and of many things – than she gives, and some may well even feel tempted to do for her what she has done here for her distinguished friend. In Venice, during a long period, for many pilgrims, Mrs Arthur Bronson, originally of New York, was, so far as society, hospitality, a charming personal welcome were concerned, almost in sole possession; she had become there, with time, quite the prime representative of those private amenities which the Anglo-Saxon abroad is apt to miss just in proportion as the place visited is publicly wonderful, and in which he therefore finds a value twice as great as at home. Mrs Bronson really earned in this way the gratitude of mingled generations and races. She sat for twenty years at the wide mouth, as it were, of the Grand Canal, holding out her hand, with endless good nature, patience, charity, to all decently accredited petitioners, the incessant troop of those either bewilderedly making or fondly renewing acquaintance with the dazzling city.

Casa Alvisi is directly opposite the high, broad-based florid church of S. Maria della Salute – so directly that from the balcony over the water-entrance your eye, crossing the canal, seems

Ludwig Johann Passini,
Mrs Bronson, 1890

to find the key-hole of the great door right in a line with it; and there was something in this position that for the time made all Venice-lovers think of the genial *padrona* as thus levying in the most convenient way the toll of curiosity and sympathy. Every one passed, every one was seen to pass, and few were those not seen to stop and to return. The most generous of hostesses died a year ago at Florence; her house knows her no more – it

Ludwig Johann Passini,
Edith Bronson, 1890

had ceased to do so for some time before her death; and the long, pleased procession – the charmed arrivals, the happy sojourns at anchor, the reluctant departures that made Ca' Alvisi, as was currently said, a social *porto di mare* – is, for remembrance and regret, already a possession of ghosts; so that, on the spot, at present, the attention ruefully averts itself from the dear little old faded but once familiarly bright façade, overtaken at last by the comparatively vulgar uses that are doing their best to "paint out" in Venice, right and left, by staring signs and other vulgarities, the immemorial note of distinction. The house, in a city of palaces, was small, but the tenant clung to her perfect, her inclusive position – the one right place that gave her a better command, as it were, than a better house obtained by a harder compromise; not being fond, moreover, of spacious halls and massive treasures, but of compact and familiar rooms, in which her remarkable accumulation of minute and delicate Venetian objects could show. She adored – in the way of the Venetian, to which all her taste addressed itself – the small, the domestic

[†]"Browning in Venice," being Recollections of the late Katherine De Kay Bronson, with a Prefatory Note by H. J. (*Cornhill Magazine*, February 1902).

Anonymous, Interior of Ca' Alvisi, c.1890

and the exquisite; so that she would have given a Tintoretto or two, I think, without difficulty, for a cabinet of tiny gilded glasses or a dinner-service of the right old silver. The general receptacle of these multiplied treasures played at any rate, through the years, the part of a friendly private-box at the constant operatic show, a box at the best point of the best tier, with the cushioned ledge of its front raking the whole scene and with its withdrawing rooms behind for more detached conversation; for easy – when not indeed slightly difficult – polyglot talk, artful *bibite*, artful cigarettes too, straight from the hand of the hostess, who could do all that belonged to a hostess, place people in relation and keep them so, take up and put down the topic, cause delicate tobacco and little gilded glasses to circulate, without ever leaving her sofa-cushions or intermitting her good nature. She exercised in these conditions, with never a block, as we say in London, in the traffic, with never an admission, an acceptance of the least social complication, her positive genius for easy interest, easy sympathy, easy friendship. It was as if, at last, she had taken the human race at large, quite irrespective of geography, for her neighbours, with neighbourly relations as a matter of course. These things, on her part, had at all events the greater appearance of ease from their having

found to their purpose – and as if the very air of Venice produced them – a cluster of forms so light and immediate, so pre-established by picturesque custom. The old bright tradition, the wonderful Venetian legend had appealed to her from the first, closing round her house and her well-plashed water-steps, where the waiting gondolas were thick, quite as if, actually, the ghost of the defunct Carnival – since I have spoken of ghosts – still played some haunting part.

Let me add, at the same time, that Mrs Bronson's social facility, which was really her great refuge from importunity, a defence with serious thought and serious feeling quietly cherished behind it, had its discriminations as well as its inveteracies, and that the most marked of all these, perhaps, was her attachment to Robert Browning. Nothing in all her beneficent life had probably made her happier than to have found herself able to minister, each year, with the returning autumn, to his pleasure and comfort. Attached to Ca' Alvisi, on the land side, is a somewhat melancholy old section of a Giustiniani palace, which she had annexed to her own premises mainly for the purpose of placing it, in comfortable guise, at the service of her friends. She liked, as she professed, when they were the real thing, to have them under her hand; and here succeeded each other, through the years, the company of the privileged and the more closely domesticated, who liked, harmlessly, to distinguish between themselves and outsiders. Among visitors partaking of this pleasant provision Mr Browning was of course easily first. But I must leave her own pen to show him as her best years knew him. The point was, meanwhile, that if her charity was great even for the outsider, this was by reason of the inner essence of it – her perfect tenderness for Venice, which she always recognised as a link. That was the true principle of fusion, the key to communication. She communicated in proportion – little or much, measuring it as she felt people more responsive or less so; and she expressed herself, or in other words her full affection for the place, only to those who had most of the same sentiment. The rich and interesting form in which she found it in Browning may well be imagined – together with the quite independent quantity of the genial at large that she also found; but I am not sure that his favor was not primarily based on his paid tribute of such things as *Two in a Gondola* and *A Toccata of Galuppi*. He has more ineffaceably than any one recorded his initiation from of old.

She was thus, all round, supremely faithful; yet it was perhaps after all with the very small folk, those to the manner born, that she made the easiest terms. She loved, she had from the first enthusiastically adopted, the engaging Venetian people, whose virtues she found touching and their infirmities but such as appeal mainly to the sense of humour and the love of anecdote; and she befriended and admired, she studied and spoiled them.

There must have been a multitude of whom it would scarce be too much to say that her long residence among them was their settled golden age. When I consider that they have lost her now I fairly wonder to what shifts they have been put and how long they may not have to wait for such another messenger of Providence. She cultivated their dialect, she renewed their boats, she piously relighted – at the top of the tide-washed *pali* of *traghetto* or lagoon – the neglected lamp of the tutelary Madonnetta; she took cognisance of the wives, the children, the accidents, the troubles, as to which she became, perceptibly, the most prompt, the established remedy. On lines where the amusement was happily less one-sided she put together

Anonymous, Mrs Bronson's household servants at Ca' Alvisi, 1888

Anonymous, Ca' Alvisi, Venice, 1888

in dialect many short comedies, dramatic proverbs, which, with one of her drawing-rooms permanently arranged as a charming diminutive theatre, she caused to be performed by the young persons of her circle – often, when the case lent itself, by the wonderful small offspring of humbler friends, children of the Venetian lower class, whose aptitude, teachability, drollery, were her constant delight. It was certainly true that an impression of Venice as humanly sweet might easily found itself on the frankness and quickness and amiability of these little people. They were at least so much to the good; for the philosophy of their patroness was as Venetian as everything else; helping her to accept experience without bitterness and to remain fresh, even in the fatigue which finally overtook her, for pleasant surprises and proved sincerities. She was herself sincere to the last for the place of her predilection; inasmuch as though she had arranged herself, in the later time – and largely for the love of "Pippa Passes" an alternative refuge at Asolo, she absented herself from Venice with continuity only under coercion of illness.

At Asolo, periodically, the link with Browning was more confirmed than weakened, and there, in old Venetian territory, and with the invasion of visitors comparatively checked, her preferentially small house became again a setting for the pleasure of talk and the sense of Italy. It contained again its own small treasures, all in the pleasant key of the homelier Venetian spirit. The plain beneath it stretched away like a purple sea from the lower cliffs of the hills, and the white *campanili* of the villages, as one was perpetually saying, showed on the expanse like scattered sails of ships. The rumbling carriage, the old-time, rattling, red-velveted carriage of provincial, rural Italy, delightful and quaint, did the office of the gondola; to Bassano, to Treviso, to high-walled Castelfranco, all pink and gold, the home of the great Giorgione. Here also memories cluster; but it is in Venice again that her vanished presence is most felt, for there, in the real, or certainly the finer, the more sifted Cosmopolis, it falls into its place among the others evoked, those of the past seekers of poetry and dispensers of romance. It is a fact that almost everyone interesting, appealing, melancholy, memorable, odd, seems at one time or another, after many days and much life, to have gravitated to Venice by a happy instinct, settling in it and treating it, cherishing it, as a sort of repository of consolations; all of which today, for the conscious mind, is mixed with its air and constitutes its unwritten history. The deposed, the defeated, the disenchanted, the wounded, or even only the bored, have seemed to find there something that no other place could give. But such people came for themselves, as we seem to see them – only with the egotism of their grievances and the vanity of their hopes. Mrs Bronson's case was beautifully different – she had come altogether for others.

EPILOGUE

The Most Beautiful of Tombs

When Henry James's Venetian essays were collected in *Italian Hours* in 1909, the expatriate Bronson-Curtis circle he had known since 1881 was no more than a memory. Mrs Bronson had been the first to go. After her daughter Edith married the Florentine Count Cosimo Rucellai in 1895 she spent less time in Ca' Alvisi than in her house in the little hill-town of Asolo so beloved by her dear friend Robert Browning. (He had immortalized it in *Pippa Passes* and his last volume of poems, *Asolando*, was dedicated to her.) "No sweeter spot, in all the sweetness of Italy, could have offered itself to old Italianised friends for confident renewals and unwitting farewells," James wrote.[1] And in April 1899, when he was staying with the Curtises at Palazzo Barbaro, he braved the forty-mile journey over bumpy country roads in the unsympathetic company of Pen Browning to spend a few days with Mrs Bronson at La Mura, her converted gate-house in the old "dismantled, dissimulated" town walls, with its extraordinary views both into the little town itself, clustered round about it, and beyond "across the great purple plain, to Bassano, Padua, Vicenza, other places, other names, charged with memories", even, on a clear morning or evening, to the Euganean Hills in the far distance. It was to be their last meeting.

Although, on his previous visit to Venice, James had left sad and disillusioned, even disgruntled – it was the late summer of 1894, thundery and, as so often in Venice at that time of year, hot and airless – he nevertheless continued to be held in thrall by the "enchantress" (as he called the city), was continually tempted to return and, always avid for "a little dear Venetian gossip", kept in touch with his friends there. In October 1898 Mrs Curtis sent him an ornament for his new home, Lamb House, Rye – "The admirable object reached me in perfect safety, and packed with a science worthy of its lustre and its history," he wrote in his letter of thanks to her on the 30th of that month,[2] going on in his convoluted manner to tell her how "handsome and picturesque" he thought it and how it gave "'importance' as the connoisseurs say, to the whole side of the room on which it so discreetly glitters. I have placed it above the chimney-piece (after trying other postures) and it consorts beautifully with the tone of the wall." He then remarked how, in his

145

Sargent, An Interior in Venice, 1899

imagination, he had climbed once again the staircase of Palazzo Barbaro and "fondly pattered" beside her "along the *sala* and into the incredible drawing room." His memory of the room was refreshed the following March when he saw Sargent's portrait group of Daniel and Ariana Curtis, their son Ralph and his wife. He "absolutely and without reserve adored it" he told Ariana,[3] who had rejected the picture as a gift from the artist. There were few paintings by Sargent that he had "ever craved more to possess" and he deplored her refusal of it. A month later he was in the room itself and doubtless repeated, in vain, his appeal to her to accept Sargent's gift.

This visit to Venice is commemorated in "Two Old Houses and Three Young Women", an essay he may have written before he returned to England (it was first published in *The Independent* 7th September 1899 and is reprinted here (see p.130) including a brief final section about Florence). A finely marked specimen of his late style – that of "James the Old Pretender" – it is written with oblique allusiveness and, unlike his earlier "travel pieces", a fastidious avoidance of factual information, which makes it read more as prose-poetry or even as fiction than as a straightforward description of the city. Proper names are discreetly veiled. Only a few initiates would have been able to identify the old houses of the title. That the first, the "high historic house with such a quantity of recorded history twinkling in the multitudinous candles" was the early sixteenth-century Palazzo Vendramin-Calergi[4] may be deduced from the reference to the *"fiançailles"* of the young lady whose "very famous paternal grandmother … had played a great part in the political history of the time and whose portrait, in the taste and dress of 1830, was conspicuous in one of the rooms." The grandmother was Caroline Duchesse de Berry who had been married to the only son of Charles X and settled in Venice when exiled from France in 1830. The young lady was Maria Carolina who was married there in 1899 to Rudolf Graf von Enzenberg – the young man described as "suffused with a fair Austrian blush". James must surely have gone to the wedding with the Curtises who were very proud of their numerous royal acquaintance, including Queen Victoria's eldest daughter, the Empress Frederick.

The un-named "three young women" of the title can be identified as Maria, Bianca and Moceniga Mocenigo – friends of both Mrs Bronson and the Curtises – by following up the reference to the record number of Doges among their forebears and to the painting described as an "exquisite specimen of an early Venetian master" in which one of their ancestors "the head of State, kneels with so sweet a dignity before the Virgin and Child" – a painting which must be that of Doge Giovanni Mocenigo, at one time attributed to Carpaccio, in the National Gallery in London. It should not, of course, be supposed that James was deliberately teasing his readers, inserting clues like the writer of a detective story. But, accustomed as he was to taking an incident from real life as the *donnée* for a story and elaborating it into general relevance, he seems to have written this essay to expand his memories into an evocation of his own personal Venice – a Venice unseen by and unknown to "cheap trippers and other aliens".

At Palazzo Barbaro in 1899 he met and struck up a friendship that was to last until death with another guest, Jessie Allen, a spinster of about his own age who lived in London. As a Christmas present in 1900 she sent him a "little brass trophy"[5] for which he "humbly, blushingly and awkwardly" thanked her. It was Venetian and "all Venice seems enclosed in its little brass parapet – and the cluster of charming objects figure to me the Salute, San Giorgio, the Dogana etc., rising out of the level lagoon," he wrote. "They are dear things – these special relics – and I love them tenderly." They wrote to each other frequently and when they were both in London gossiped over tea at her house in Eaton Terrace – exchanging, Sargent said, "mischievous tattle"[6] about the Curtises and other mutual friends.

Palazzo Barbaro was often in James's mind at that time while he pondered *The Wings of the Dove* in which he transformed it no more than nominally into Palazzo Leporelli. For this novel about a rich young woman with a love of life condemned to death by some mysterious ailment and fastening her affection on a young man who cannot reciprocate, he had sketched a full outline[7] in a notebook in November 1894 – that is to say, some five months after the end of the visit to Venice following Fenimore Woolson's suicide. Surprisingly, but perhaps significantly, he then saw "Nice or Mentone – or Cairo – or Corfu – designated as the scene of the action," practically anywhere other than Venice. By the time he came to write – or, rather, dictate – the novel in 1901 (he began it in July and finished it within a year) he had, however, recognized that his heroine, the sad, beautiful, doomed Milly Theale could pass the last months of her short life only in the "most melancholy of cities" which, he had written earlier, was "the most beautiful of tombs. Nowhere else has the past been laid to rest with such tenderness, such sadness of resignation and remembrance."

Drawing on a treasury of memories gathered in the course of three decades, James conjured up a vision of Venice that envelopes his protagonists like a mist rising from the lagoon. Milly asks for accommodation "at Venice, please, if possible, no dreadful, no vulgar hotel; but, if it can at all be managed – you know what I mean – some fine old rooms, wholly independent, for a series of months. Plenty of them too, and the more interesting the better: part of a palace, historic and picturesque, but strictly inodorous, where we shall be to ourselves, with a cook, don't you know? – with servants, frescoes,

tapestries, antiquities, the thorough make-believe of a settlement."[8] She took possession "gratefully glad that the warmth of the Southern summer was still in the high florid rooms, palatial chambers where hard cool pavements took reflections in their lifelong polish, and where the sun on the stirred sea-water, flickered up through open windows, played over the painted 'subjects' in the splendid ceilings – medallions of purple and brown, of brave old melancholy colour, medals as of old reddened gold, embossed and beribboned, all toned with time and all flourished and scolloped and gilded about, set in their great moulded and figured concavity."[9] The owners, "charming people, conscious Venice-lovers, evidently, had given up their house to her, and had fled to a distance, to other countries, to hide their blushes alike over what they had, however briefly, alienated, and over what they had, however durably, gained."[10]

Just so did the Curtises let Palazzo Barbaro to summer tenants, notably Isabella Stewart Gardner with whom, as we have seen, James stayed there one summer. And in Milly Theale there are traits not only of James's beloved cousin Minnie Temple, who died young, and Fenimore Woolson, who died in Venice, but also of the irrepressibly volatile Mrs Gardner whom he had described as a "forlorn, bereft, emaciated lady" when introducing her to Mrs Bronson in 1884. There is an uncanny similarity between a portrait of Mrs Gardner in Venice by Ludwig Passini, who had also painted Mrs Bronson, and the description of Milly Theale in a white dress with a "long priceless chain"[11] of pearls that "wound twice round the neck, hung, heavy and pure, down the front of the wearer's breast – so far down that Milly's trick, evidently unconscious, of holding and vaguely fingering and entwining a part of it, conduced presumably to convenience."

There are elements of James himself in Merton Densher, the young journalist with whom Milly has fallen in love. Both had the same dislike of Venetian hotels – "the establishment, choked at that season with the polyglot herd, cockneys of all climes, mainly German, mainly American, mainly English, it appeared as the corresponding sensitive nerve was touched, sounded loud and sweet, sounded anything and everything but Italian, but Venetian."[12] Densher took rooms with "ancient rickety objects too refined in their shabbiness, amiable in their decay," not, indeed, where James had stayed in 1881 but near the Rialto where he had visited one memorable summer night the rooms of Herbert Pratt. He strolled "through dusky labyrinthine alleys and empty *campi*, overhung with mouldering palaces, where … the sound of a rare footfall on the enclosed pavement was like that of a retarded dancer in a banquet-hall deserted."[13] The atmosphere becomes increasingly portentous and at a crucial moment in the story, a "Venice all of evil"[14] breaks out, "a Venice of cold lashing rain from a low black sky, of wicked wind raging through the narrow passes, of general arrest and interruption, with the people engaged in all the water-life huddled, stranded and wageless, bored and cynical, under archways and bridges." In the Piazza "there were stretches of the gallery paved with squares of red marble, greasy now with the salt spray; and the whole place, in its huge elegance, the grace of its conception and the beauty of its detail, was more than ever like a great drawing-room, the drawing-room of Europe, profaned and bewildered by some reverse of fortune. The tables and chairs that overflowed from the cafés were gathered, still with a pretence of service, into the arcade, and here and there a spectacled German, with his coat-collar up, partook publicly of food and philosophy."

While working on *The Wings of the Dove* James took time off to write his tribute to the memory of Mrs Bronson, published in the *Cornhill Magazine* in February 1902. Her death had, he told her daughter, made him feel older and sadder. "It is the end of so many things – so many delightful memories, histories, associations – some of the happiest elements of one's own past. It breaks into my tenderness, even for the dear old Italy and seems to alter and overshadow that cherished relation."[15] And now, once again, his "melancholy days in Venice" after Fenimore Woolson's suicide came back to him as they had done, continually, ever since that agonized spring, renewed even by such a trivial piece of news as that of the death of the dog she had owned. He was not to return to Venice or indeed to Italy at all until 1907.

Sargent, Henry James, 1913

Sunshine Captured and Held

During these years of absence James may well have had news of Venice from Sargent, whom he met frequently in London where they were both inveterate diners-out, much though they both complained of social entanglements. For they were "real friends" William Graham Robertson[1] was to write, "they understood each other perfectly and their points of view were in many ways identical. Renegade Americans both, each did his best to love his country and failed far more signally than did the average Englishman: they were *plus anglais que les Anglais* with an added fastidiousness and mental remoteness that was not English." And their similar responses to Venice may perhaps have been conditioned by their position as expatriates who had become true cosmopolitans, able to make themselves at home wherever they wished yet always viewing their European surroundings with a certain detachment, with a poised equanimity which Sargent was to catch perfectly in his portrait of James.

Anonymous photograph of Mrs Curtis and Ralph Curtis in the Salone, Palazzo Barbaro, c.1910

Sargent went to Venice nearly every year and in 1898, as a token of his gratitude to the Curtises for their great hospitality over the years and also as an act of homage to the glory and grandeur of Venetian life in which he now so willingly indulged, he portrayed his hosts in the great rich *salone* of Palazzo Barbaro (see p.146) with its three enormous paintings by eighteenth-century Venetian masters inset in the flamboyant stucco decorations and with its Venetian rococo furniture of the type he loved, painted and gilded, rather roughly made perhaps but so much more sensual and sunny than French eighteenth-century furniture. Mrs Curtis, however, rejected the picture. She would not accept it as a gift.[2] Her son Ralph's lackadaisical pose was, she thought, indecorous and, moreover, she had been made to look

Sargent, Rococo Mirror,
1898

too old (she was then sixty-six). Whistler scorned it, "smudge everywhere",[3] and compared its free handling with the "finish, the delicacy, the elegance, the repose" of Dutch seventeenth-century interiors (a strange comment from the painter of *nocturnes*!). But, as we have seen, Henry James coveted it. And Sargent himself was well enough satisfied to hand it down to posterity as his Royal Academy diploma piece, discreetly entitled *An Interior in Venice*. Nor does he seem to have harboured any grudge against Ariana Curtis for refusing it.

"The Barbaro is a sort of Fontaine de Jouvence, for it sends one back twenty years, besides making the present remarkably all right," he wrote after staying with the Curtises in 1898. *An Interior in Venice*, with its free brushwork and its informal composition is, indeed, closer to the masterly groups of children he had painted at the beginning of his career than to his more recent icons of professional society beauties and ladies of fashion. It is one of his finest works, and sums up in a way no other artist was able to do, a whole epoch in American expatriate life – that refined and highly civilized little society which formed the subject of so many of Henry James's novels and short stories. But many views of Venice he painted in oils and, especially, watercolours on his almost annual visits from the late 1890s until 1913 could hardly differ more sharply from those of the early 1880s.

Sargent reverted to none of his low-life genre subjects: gondoliers are virtually the only Venetians that appear in these later paintings and they are, as often as not, either resting or sleeping. Nor did he seek out any remote cavernous alleys or insalubrious small canals. In Venice, Sargent was on holiday, far from the studio in Tite Street where one sitter followed another on the posing platform. Time and again he vowed to give up the work that had brought him fame and fortune. "No more paughtraits," he told Ralph Curtis at one of these moments.[4] "I abhor and adjure them and hope never to paint another especially of the upper classes." He wanted to devote himself entirely, if possible, to the historical and allegorical wall and ceiling paintings commissioned for the Boston Public Library, begun in 1893 but not finished until 1916; and from this vast undertaking he needed occasional respite. Nearly every summer he travelled on the European continent, painting, as a friend remarked, only what he had a mind to. After his mother's death in 1906 he was always accompanied by his unmarried sister Emily, usually by his other sister Violet, her husband and their increasing family as well as by various friends, notably the painter Wilfred von Glehn and his wife, who was a distant cousin of Henry James. Their daylight hours were spent in painting and posing in a light-hearted mood. Jane von Glehn referred to a "most amusing and killingly funny picture" Sargent was painting of her on one of these trips.[5] In one of Sargent's Venetian watercolours she appears seated in a gondola beside her husband who is carefully sketching among the shipping on the Giudecca Canal. In an oil painting worked up in the studio from studies made on the spot and a photograph, but retaining an appearance of complete spontaneity, Sargent depicted his sisters in a gondola gliding beneath the Rialto Bridge –

Sargent, Sketching on the Giudecca, c.1904

Sargent, The Rialto, Venice, c.1911

the record of a treasured moment in a Venetian holiday.

The sun is always shining brightly in these late views, as on one of those days evoked by Henry James when "Venice glowed and plashed and called and chimed again: the air was like a clap of hands, and the scattered pinks, yellows, blues, sea-greens, were like a hanging out of vivid stuffs, a laying down of fine carpets."[6] Such moments could best be caught in bright watercolour pigment dashingly applied in translucent washes. A large proportion of the watercolours Sargent painted between 1900 and 1913 are of Venice. Although he kept some for himself, he exhibited and sold others. He also negotiated the sale of groups, including Venetian views, to American museums, which suggests that he set some store by them for his posthumous reputation. They seem, nevertheless, to be completely spontaneous, quite unpremeditated, the result simply of an irrepressible urge to record the fleeting impressions that delighted his eye as he relaxed with his sisters and with old and new friends. As one of his new friends, and future biographer, Evan Charteris, wrote: "He followed his own

Anonymous photograph of Emily Sargent and Eliza Wedgwood, Venice, c.1911

pleasure; every picture is the offspring of exultation in his facility; their spontaneity is pronounced, they flow from his hand with the turbulence of water from a mill-race. If little is added to what he represents, nothing is taken away. If the scenes he painted delight us, the same delight will be found in his renderings of them. To live with Sargent's watercolours is to live with sunshine captured and held, with the lustre of a bright and legible world, 'the refluent shade' and the ambient ardours of the noon'."[7]

Sure of himself, Sargent no longer felt any need to seek out unusual subjects to display his originality.

Although he continued to frequent the small canals, he was no longer inhibited from painting such famous and often depicted buildings as the Salute and the Doges' Palace. Nor, of course, was Claude Monet, whom Sargent had known for years and who made his only visit to Venice in the autumn of 1908,[8] staying for the first few days in Palazzo Barbaro as the guest of their mutual friend Mrs Charles Hunter, who had rented it from the Curtises. The view from the steps of Palazzo Barbaro's canal entrance, looking down the Grand Canal towards the Salute, was the subject of several of the paintings Monet began in Venice – "*des essais, des commencements*", he called them, for he finished few if any during his three months stay. They were worked up later in his studio in Giverny in northern France where he recalled nostalgically the "unique light" that had so immediately captivated him in Venice. Completed by 1912, when he exhibited the whole series in Paris, his Venetian paintings are a peculiar synthesis of observation and recollection – evocations, suffused with the warm glow of memory but veiled as if they were a distant souvenir – like, indeed,

Sargent, The Libreria, 1904

Sargent, Venetian Canal, c.1910

Monet, Santa Maria della Salute, 1908-12

many of the descriptions written by James and also by Marcel Proust whose memories of Venice and of Monet's paintings merged into a single vision.

But, quite unlike Monet who dissolved the stones of Venice in a bath of radiant light, Sargent not only painted the well-known buildings he had ignored in his earlier work but sharply focused attention on their sculptural decorations. The baroque statues on the façade of the Salute and those on the eighteenth-century church of the Gesuati, for instance, caught his attention – as did the grandiloquent water-entrances of palaces with their gaily and spirally painted mooring-posts and sea-weedy, slippery steps. One of his views is of the eighteenth-century church of San Geremia and Palazzo Labia which enshrines masterly frescoes by Tiepolo (an artist he greatly admired). For Sargent shared with such friends as Vernon Lee, Mrs Gardner and Edith Wharton, a taste for the then unfashionable *settecento*, its buildings, paintings, furniture, glass and maiolica as well as its music and literature.[9] And Henry James, too, was attracted to the Venetian eighteenth-century world of Browning's "A Toccato of Galuppis".[10]

Many of these paintings are, however, centred on watercraft, the humble *sandali* used for transporting merchandise, gondolas, of course, with gondoliers posed in the rhythmical swing of their rowing, patterns of brightly coloured sails and complicated rigging, and usually in the distance steamers off the Molo or in the Giudecca Canal. However, no puffing and hooting vaporetti are allowed to mar the idyllic scene. For although he had changed since his first visit and developed new artistic interests, the Venice he depicted and loved was for him to remain unchanged – as he had first seen it. He averted his brush from buildings that had been newly erected or harshly restored. Gazing above the crowds of tourists in the Piazzetta he focused on the richly sculptured upper storey of Sansovino's library. Not until 1913 did he find the city so spoiled by "swarms of smart Londoners"[11] that he never returned.

The Spell of the Enchantress

James also clung to the Venice he had first known. He was brought back to it in 1905 when revising *The Portrait of a Lady* for re-publication in the New York edition of his works. Recalling his stay on the Riva degli Schiavoni where he finished the novel in 1881, he wrote: "There are pages of the book which, in the reading over, have seemed to make me see again the bristling curve of the wide Riva, the large colour-spots of the balconied houses and the repeated undulation of the little hunchbacked bridges, marked by the rise and drop again, with the wave, of foreshortened clicking pedestrians. The Venetian footfall and the Venetian cry – all talk there, wherever uttered, having the pitch of a call across the water – come in once more at the window, renewing one's old impression of the delighted senses and the divided, frustrated mind."[1] He had also to draw lovingly on his memories when giving instructions to Alvin Langdon Coburn[2] about the subjects to be photographed in Venice for the frontispieces to two of the twenty-three volumes.

For the frontispiece to the second volume of *The Wings of the Dove* James said that he had "vaguely in mind the Palazzo Barbaro". It could be seen from the Accademia Bridge, he told Coburn, "the very old Gothic one. Only one palace, the Franchetti, a great big sort of yellow-faced restored one, with vast

Muster-Böhm photograph,
Ponte dell' Accademia,
c. 1910

Gothic windows and balcony, intervenes between it and the said iron bridge." (The iron bridge by the English engineer Neville was opened in 1854. It was replaced by the present wooden structure in 1932.) James wanted Coburn's photograph to show the beautiful range of old "*upper* Gothic windows, those attached to the part of the palace concerned in my story". But if this proved impossible, Coburn might "try some other palace, or simply try some other right range of palaces, in some other reach or stretch of the Canal … yet especially *not* choosing the pompous and obvious things that one everywhere sees photos of." Coburn obliged with a shot of the facade of Palazzo Barbaro, apparently taken from water-level.

Alvin Langdon Coburn, Frontispiece for The Wings of the Dove, 1906

The frontispiece for the volume in which *The Aspern Papers* was to be included presented more complicated problems. James wanted a photograph of Ca' Capello on Rio Marin which he had had in mind as the home of Juliana Bordereau and her niece. "Your best way to get to the Rio Marin will be to obtain guidance, for a few coppers, from some alert Venetian street-boy (or of course you can go, romantically, in a gondola)," he told Coburn on 16th December 1906. "But the extremely tortuous and complicated walk – taking Piazza San Marco as a starting point – will show you so much, so many bits and odds and ends, such a revel of Venetian picturesqueness, that I advise your doing it on foot as much as possible." Then he remembered that it would be easier to take the *vaporetto* to the station, only a few minutes' walk from the Rio Marin. "It is the old pink-faced, battered-looking and quite homely and plain (as things go in Venice) old Palazzino on the right of the small canal, a little way along as you enter it by the end of the canal towards the station. It has a garden behind it, and I think, though I am not sure, some bit of a garden wall beside it; it doesn't moreover bathe its steps, if I remember right, directly in the canal, but has a small Riva or footway in front of it, and *then* water-steps down from this little quay. As to that, however, the time since I have seen it may muddle me; but I am almost sure." He said that Coburn must judge for himself how suitable it was as a subject for a photograph and in a sentence which only the Master himself could have dictated: "I think it *must*, more or less, or sufficiently, with or without such adjuncts of the rest of the scene (from the bank opposite, from the bank near, or from wherever you can damnably manage it) as may seem to contribute or complete – to be needed, in short, for the interesting effect." His own preference was for an interior view of the central *sala* or *portego* looking towards the garden end, or for the garden itself. But if neither was satisfactory Coburn was to wander about until he found an alternative: "something that looks sufficiently like it, some old second-rate palace on a by-canal with a Riva in front." When Coburn went to Palazzo Cappello, however, he took instead of the views specified an artistically effective photograph of a potted tree in the rather plain *cortile*, barely recognizable as Venetian except to those familiar with the secluded corners of the city. (Now, in 1989, the palace and its garden, inhabited only by cats, are in such a deplorable state that the precise viewpoint cannot be identified.) As softly focused as James's later descriptions of the city, it was

*Alvin Langdon Coburn,
Frontispiece for The
Aspern Papers, 1906*

entitled "Juliana's Court" and used as the frontispiece to *The Aspern Papers*. Other photographs he took at the time, notably one of a bridge and its reflection in a small canal were much more characteristically Venetian – perhaps thought by James too "obvious" for his purpose.

Coburn was extremely brisk and lost no time in Venice. He later recorded that never before or since had he felt so miserably cold and damp – until he moved into "a German pension with enormous stoves and old-fashioned feather beds".[3] By the end of December he was back in London with his photographs and on 2nd January 1907 James wrote to tell him that they had had a "huge success with my highly tasteful friends last p.m.";[4] he wanted to buy prints of them all for himself. Awakening old memories, they may well have stimulated a desire to return to Venice. After staying with Edith Wharton in Paris and joining her on a motor-tour, he went first to Rome (partly to see Henrik Andersen, the uncanny avatar of his own *Roderick Hudson* whom he had first encountered in 1899). But Rome had been ruined – "the abatements and changes and modernism and vulgarities, the crowd and the struggle and the frustration (of real communion with what one wanted) are quite dreadful – and I really quite revel in the thought that I shall never come to Italy *at all* again – in all probability," he told his nephew William.[5] Florence had also been vulgarized, he found. In comparison, Venice had hardly changed at all: indeed he thought it "more characteristically exquisite and loveable" than ever.[6] He stayed at Palazzo Barbaro with the Curtises, who were "kindness and hospitality unlimited", he told Jessie Allen, and "every note strikes true from the cool dim dawn, when the canal is a great curly floor of dark grim marble, till the cooler blue night" when he went out in the gondola "to be cradled by the plash outside the Giudecca." There were serious disadvantages: Daniel Curtis always rather bored him, but he and his wife had both become more prejudiced than ever. They now had "such a terror of the vulgar" that they "discriminated so invidiously against anyone I might weakly wish to see, of my little other promiscuous acquaintances in Venice, that I felt that I could never again face the irritation and inconvenience of it." And yet, and yet, as he was preparing to leave, he once again sensed "the heartbreak it is just to feel this enchantress (I allude now to the terrible old Venice herself!) weave her spell just again supremely to lose her. One dreams again of some clutched perch of one's own here." He was never to see Venice again.

Alvin Langdon Coburn, The White Bridge, 1906

NOTES

This book owes much to the publications of Leon Edel, his five volume biography of Henry James (*The Untried Years* 1953, *The Conquest of London* 1962, *The Middle Years* 1963, *The Treacherous Years* 1969 and *The Master* 1972) and to his editions of the letters and notebooks of Henry James, see abbreviated titles below. For Henry James and Italy we are indebted to C. Giorcelli, *Henry James e l'Italia* (Rome 1968), and C. Maves, *Sensuous Pessimism:Italy in the Work of Henry James* (Bloomington, Indiana 1973); for Henry James and Venice to M. Battilana, *Venezia sfondo e simbolo nella narrativa de Henry James* (Milan 1971, 1987); S. Perosa (ed.), *Henry James e Venezia* (Florence 1987) and Rosella Mamoli Zorzi (ed.), *Henry James. Lettere da Palazzo Barbaro* (Milan 1989). For Whistler, general biographical as well as more technical information has been derived from Katherine A. Lochlan, *The Etchings of James McNeill Whistler* (New Haven and London 1984), Margaret MacDonald, *Notes, Harmonies and Nocturnes* (New York 1984), Denys Sutton, *Nocturne. The Art of James McNeill Whistler* (London 1963) and *James McNeill Whistler* (London 1966) and Andrew McLaren Young et al., *The Paintings of James McNeill Whistler* (London 1980) as well as the earlier sources cited in the following notes; for Sargent much is owed to Patricia Hills (ed.), *John Singer Sargent* (New York 1986), Stanley Olson, *John Singer Sargent His Portrait* (London 1986), Richard Ormond, *John Singer Sargent* (New York 1970), Carter Ratcliffe, *John Singer Sargent* (New York 1982). For Whistler, Sargent and other artists in Venice the following exhibition catalogues have been invaluable: Denys Sutton, *Venice Rediscovered* (Wildenstein, London 1972), Donna Seldon, *Americans in Venice 1879-1913* (Coe Kerr Gallery, New York 1983), Giuseppe Pavanello and Giandomenico Romanelli (eds.), *Venezia nell'Ottocento* (Museo Correr, Venice 1983-4), Margaretta M. Lovell, *Venice the American View 1860-1920* (Fine Arts Museum of San Francisco 1985), Denys Sutton, *John Singer Sargent* (Isetan Museum of Art, Tokyo 1989).

The following abbreviations are used in the notes for frequently cited sources:
Edel Letters – Leon Edel (ed.), *Henry James Letters* (Cambridge, Mass., vol I (1974), II (1975), III (1980), IV (1984)).
Edel Notebooks – Leon Edel and Lyall N. Powers (eds.), *The Complete Notebooks of Henry James* (New York 1987).
New York edition – *The Novels and Tales of Henry James*, New York edition (New York and London, 24 volumes 1907-9).

FIRST IMPRESSIONS: HENRY JAMES

1 *Edel Letters* vol II p.355.
2 Edouard Manet visited Venice in late 1874 and a contemporary later said, *"Les lagunes, les palais, les vieilles maisons décrépitées et patinées par le temps lui offraient des motifs inépuisables. Mais, de préférence, il recherchait les coins peu connus."* However, only two Venetian paintings by Manet are known and both are of the Grand Canal, cf. F. Cachin et al., Manet (Exhibition Catalogue, Grand Palais, Paris 1983 pp. 373-6); J. Wilson-Bareau, "L'Année Impressioniste de Manet: Argenteuil et Venise en 1874" in *Revue de l'Art* no. 86, 1989, pp.28-34. For Renoir and Monet in Venice (see pp 43, 58, 59, 157-159, 166, 169).
3 William Dean Howells, *Venetian Life*, 1867 (London 1907 p.141).
4 *Edel Letters* (vol I p.134).
5 *Edel Letters* (vol I p.128).
6 *Venise, Guide Historique* (Trieste 1861 p.256) refers to *"Albergo Palazzo Zucchelli, corte Barozzi, propriété de M. Auguste Barbesi, où il n'y a que des chambres à louer. N.2161"*. A restaurant had evidently been added before 1869. The building is now part of the Hotel Europa e Regina.
7 *Edel Letters* (vol I p.134).
8 *Edel Letters* (vol I p.136-44).
9 James followed Ruskin's erroneous spelling "San Cassano".
10 Théophile Gautier, *Italia*, 1852 (Paris 1876 p.127): *"Quelles belles épaules blanches! quelles nuques blondes aux nattes enroulées! quels bras ronds et charmants! quel sourire d'éternelle jeunesse dans cette toile merveileuse, où Paul Véronèse semble avoir dit son dernier mot! Ciel, nuages, arbres, fleurs, terrains, mer, carnation, draperies, tout parait trempé dans la lumière d'un Elysée inconnu."*
11 *Edel Letters* (vol I p.145).
12 *Travelling Companions*, reprinted in Leon Edel (ed.), *The Complete Tales of Henry James* (vol II London 1962 pp.171-225).
13 *Edel Letters* (vol I p.296).
14 "Venice: An Early Impression". The essay, then entitled "A European Summer VII – From Venice to Stras-

bourg", was first published in *The Nation* XVI, January to June 1873 (6 March 1873 pp.163-5) and reprinted in *Henry James, Transatlantic Sketches* (Boston 1875) with a very few minor alterations (e.g. "decease" for "decline", "was" for "is"). When he prepared the copy for *Italian Hours* (London 1909), however, he not only adopted English spelling but also made alterations to improve the wording on every page. Where, for example, he had first written of a stay in Venice: "this, I consider, is to be as happy as one may safely be", he now wrote: "...as happy as is consistent with the preservation of reason". He likened the children at Torcello to "Abyssinians" in 1873 but to "cannibals" in 1909. The passage on Tintoretto had originally ended with the words: "...his life – and a very intense one" for which he substituted: "...his life – one of the most intellectually passionate ever led." The text printed here is that in *Italian Hours*.

15 John L. Sweeney, *The Painter's Eye. Notes and Essays on the Pictorial Arts* by Henry James (London 1956 p.21).

16 Henry James, "Recent Florence" in *Atlantic Monthly* May 1878 reprinted in *Italian Hours* (London 1909 p.129).

A VENICE IN VENICE: WHISTLER

1 Katherine A.Lochman, *The Etchings of James McNeill Whistler* (New Haven and London 1984, p.182).

2 ibid p.183.

3 James McNeill Whistler, "Mr Whistler's Ten o'clock" (London 1888, p.15).

4 Otto Bacher, *With Whistler in Venice* (New York 1908 p.97).

5 For William Graham's friendship with Whistler in Venice see Andrew McLaren Young et al., *The Paintings of James McNeill Whistler* (New Haven and London 1980 pp.122-24).

6 Otto Bacher op. cit. p.4.

7 For Henry James on Duveneck and the Bootts, see Edel, *Henry James, The Conquest of London* (London 1962 p.406).

8 Letter to Luke Fildes in *L.V. Fildes, A Victorian Painter* (Luke Fildes) quoted by Denys Sutton, *Nocturne: The Art of James McNeill Whistler* (London 1963 pp.92-3).

9 Letter from Ralph Curtis in E.R. and J.Pennell, *The Life of James McNeill Whistler* (London and Philadelphia 1908 vol. I pp.272-5). For the Curtises see Rosella Mamoli Zorzi (ed.), *Henry James. Lettere da Palazzo Barbaro* (Milan 1989).

For Mrs Bronson see M. Meredith (ed.), *More than Friend. The Letters of Robert Browning to Katherine De Kay Bronson* (Baylor University, Kansas 1985).

10 One of Twachtman's Venetian pastels is reproduced in Margaret Lovell, *Venice, The American View 1860-1920* (Fine Arts of Museum of San Francisco 1985 no.86).

11 E.R. and J.Pennell op. cit. p.263.

12 Mortimer Mempes, *Whistler as I Knew Him* (London 1904 pp.22-23).

13 Walter Richard Sickert "The New Life of Whistler" 1908, reprinted in Osbert Sitwell (ed.) *A Free House* (London 1947 p.13).

14 Otto Bacher op. cit. pp.55-56.

15 K.A.Lochnan op. cit. pp.187.

16 Otto Bacher op. cit. pp.75-76.

17 "Palace in Rags", private collection, reproduced in Margaret F. MacDonald, *Notes, Harmonies & Nocturnes, Small Works by James McNeill Whistler*, Exhibition Catalogue, M. Knoedler & Co. (New York 1984 no.88).

18 Margaret F. MacDonald, "Lines on a Venetian Lagoon" in L. D. Cheney and P. G. Marks (eds.), *The Whistler Papers* (Lowell Mass. 1986 p.4).

19 ibid p.7.

20 E. W. Godwin in *The British Architect* February 1881.

21 *Edel Letters* vol II p.167.

22 J. L. Sweeney op. cit. p.174.

PAR TEMPS GRIS: SARGENT

1 Richard Ormond, *John Singer Sargent* (New York 1970 p.85).

2 ibid p.29.

3 Richard Ormond op. cit. p.30.

4 Renoir mentions meeting Whistler in Paris that spring before leaving for Venice, see M. Florisoone, "Renoir et la Famille Charpentier: Lettres Inédits" in *L'Amour de l'Art* (XIX 1938 pp.31-40).

5 B. E. White, "Renoir's trip to Italy" in *Art Bulletin* (LI 1969 pp.333-351).

6 V. Lee, *Studies of the Eighteenth Century in Italy* (London 1880 p.265).

7 Linda Ayres "Sargent in Venice" in Patricia Hills (ed.) *John Singer Sargent* Exhibition Catalogue, Whitney Museum of American Art (New York 1986-7 p.67).

8 Arthur Baignères, "Première Exposition de la Société

Internationale des Peintres et Sculpteurs" in *Gazette des Beaux Arts* (XXVII 1883 p.192).

9   Henry James, "John Singer Sargent" in *Harper's Monthly Magazine* 75 (October 1887 p.689).

DELIGHTED SENSES AND DIVIDED MIND

1   *Edel Notebooks* (p.220).

2   Jeanne Clegg, *Ruskin and Venice* (London 1981 p.147).

3   In 1887 he said that he was distressed that the "poor little Montenegro" had been unkindly mentioned in a gossipy account of Italian society by May Marcy McLellan in the *New York World* (*Edel Letters* vol III p.155) though there is no direct reference to her in the only such article that has been traced (of 14 November 1886). In an undated letter to Ariana Curtis written from Lamb House (i.e. after 1897) he remarked that the "poor little princess" might be made the point of departure for a story (Rosella Mamoli Zorzi (ed.), *Henry James. Lettere da Palazzo Barbaro* Milan 1989 p.xxix).

4   *Edel Notebooks* (p.221).

5   Preface to *The Portrait of a Lady* (New York edition vol III p.v).

6   *Edel Notebooks* (p.222).

7   Leon Edel (ed.), *Henry James. Selected Letters* (Cambridge Mass. 1987 p.197).

8   *Edel Letters* (vol II p.388).

9   New York edition (vol VI pp.141-146).

10   *Edel Letters* (vol III pp.166-7).

11   ibid pp.170-171.

12   I. Cooper Willis (ed.), *Vernon Lee's Letters*, quoted in J. Lomax and R. Ormond, *John Singer Sargent and the Edwardian Age* (Exhibition Catalogue National Portrait Gallery, London 1979 p.30).

13   *Edel Letters* (vol III p.175).

14   ibid p.188.

15   *Edel Notebooks* (pp.33-34).

16   Preface to *The Aspern Papers* (New York edition vol XII p.xi).

17   See Van Wyck Brooks, *The Dream of Arcadia* (London 1958 p.257) and Rosella Mamoli Zorzi (op. cit. pp.112-113).

18   New York edition (vol XII p.9).

19   ibid p.16.

20   New York edition (vol XI p.556). *The Pupil* was first published in 1891. In another story of the same year, *The Chaperon* (New York edition vol X pp.437-500) the turning-point is set in Venice.

21   New York edition (vol XI p.76).

22   ibid p.51.

23   ibid p.110.

24   *Edel Letters* (vol III p.287).

25   Maisie Ward, *Robert Browning and His World: Two Robert Brownings?* (London 1969 p.255).

26   *Edel Letters* (vol III p.287).

27   M. Ward op. cit. p.297.

28   Sargent's portrait of Mrs Gardner is in the Isabella Stewart Gardner Museum, Boston.

29   Louise Hall Tharp, *Mrs Jack* (Boston 1965 p.161).

30   *Edel Letters* (vol III p.390).

31   Vernon Lee, *Vanitas* (London 1892 pp.7-119).

32   R. D. Yeazell (ed.), *The Death and Letters of Alice James* (Berkeley 1981 p.149). James wrote a laudatory essay about her for *Harper's Weekly* in 1887 reprinted as "Miss Woolson" in his *Partial Portraits* (London 1888). For her see Joan Myers Weimer (ed.), Constance Fenimore Woolson, *Women Artists, Women Exiles. "Miss Grief" and Other Stories* (New Brunswick & London 1988).

33   *Edel Letters* (vol III p.467).

34   ibid p.465.

35   ibid p.476.

36   James's account was recalled by Mrs Huntington for a BBC programme in 1956, see Alide Cagidimetrio in S. Perosa (ed.), *Henry James e Venezia* (Florence 1987 pp.54-55).

37   R. M. Zorzi op. cit. p.63.

FOUR ESSAYS FROM ITALIAN HOURS

Venice, The Grand Canal, Two Old Houses and Three Young Women and *Casa Alvisi* were first published in various periodicals between 1882 and 1902. They are reprinted here from the texts established by James for publication in *Italian Hours*. He wrote, "I have not hesitated to amend my text, expressively, wherever it seemed urgently to ask for this…"

Venice was first published in *Century Magazine XXV* (November 1882 pp.3-23) and reprinted in *Henry James, Portraits of Places* (London 1883). In 1909 he made numerous alterations. On page after page he changed the pronoun for Venice from the neuter to the feminine. "The fault of Venice is that, though it is easy to admire it, it is not easy to live in it", for instance, was transformed into: "the fault of Venice is that, though she is easy to admire, she is not so easy to live with as you count living in other places". It has been suggested that the use of the feminine pronoun reflected James's "eroticization" of Venice. But numerous other English and American writers have referred to Venice in the feminine and the name in Italian and French (*Venezia* and *Venise*) is feminine.

Most of the alterations James made were small and clearly intended simply to smoothe the prose. In the last paragraph of the fourth section, however, he amended the wording for other reasons, to qualify his remarks about the Venetian "race". "It has not a genius for morality", he had originally written, "It scruples not to represent the false as the true, and is liable to confusion in the attribution of property." This was amended to read: "It hasn't a genius for stiff morality… It scruples but scantly to represent the false as the true, and has been accused of cultivating the occasion to grasp and overreach, and of steering a crooked course – not to your and my advantage – amid the sanctities of property."

The Grand Canal was first published in *Scribner's Magazine XII* (November 1892 pp.531-50) and in *Great Streets of the World* (New York and London 1892) together with essays by R. H. David, W. E. Story, Andrew Lang and others. It had illustrations after drawings by a contemporary Venetian artist, Alessandro Zezzos. When he prepared the essay for reprinting in *Italian Hours* James made no more than a few very minor alterations. In the first paragraph, for instance, he had originally written "if the Grand Canal, however, is not quite technically a 'street', the perverted Piazza is perhaps even less of one" and altered this to read "…even less normal". James seems to have been unaware of a mistake that he made at the end where he accused Canaletto of depicting the church of San Simeone Profeta "on the wrong side of the Canal". He surely had in mind the picture in the National Gallery, London, showing this church and that of the Scalzi but erroneously supposed that the view was painted looking towards the Rialto. Canaletto's view, in fact, was painted in the other direction and records the buildings that were demolished in the mid-nineteenth century to make way for the railway station.

Two Old Houses and Three Young Women was first published in *The Independent LI* (7 September 1899 pp.406-412) and reprinted in 1909 without significant alteration.

Casa Alvisi was first printed in *Cornhill Magazine n.s. XII* (February 1902 pp.145-149) as the introduction to Katherine De Kay Bronson's posthumously published reminiscences of Robert Browning in Venice. Only the first words were changed for publication on its own in the *American Critic XL* (February 1902 pp.162-164) and no further alterations were made when it was reprinted in *Italian Hours*.

EPILOGUE

THE MOST BEAUTIFUL OF TOMBS

1   Henry James, *William Wetmore Story and His Friends*, (Edinburgh and London 1903 vol II pp.282-3).
2   R. M. Zorzi op. cit. p.66.
3   Stanley Olson, *John Singer Sargent His Portrait* (London 1986 p.218).
4   Identified by Mirella Battilana Shankorsky, *"Sei Personaggi in cerca di nome"* in *Ateneo Veneto N.S. X* (1972 pp.217-230).
5   *Edel Letters* (vol IV p.174).
6   Leon Edel, *Henry James: The Master* (London 1972 p.162).
7   *Edel Notebooks* (pp.102-7).
8   New York edition (vol XX p.134-5).
9   ibid. p.132.
10   ibid. p.135.
11   ibid. p.217.
12   ibid. p.171.
13   ibid. p.183.
14   ibid. p.259 ff.
15   *Edel Letters* (vol IV p.183).

SUNSHINE CAPTURED AND HELD

1   William Graham Robertson, *Life Was Worth Living* (London 1931).
2   Evan Charteris, *John Sargent* (London 1927 p.163).
3   E. R. and J. Pennell, *The Whistler Journal* (Philadelphia 1921 p.39).
4   Evan Charteris op. cit. p.155.
5   P. Hills (ed.), *John Singer Sargent Exhibition Catalogue*

(Whitney Museum of American Art New York 1986-87 p.191).

6   New York edition (vol XX p.294).

7   Evan Charteris op. cit. p.225.

8   See H. Adhémar et al, *Homage à Claude Monet Exhibition Catalogue* (Grand Palais Paris 1980 pp.120-122).

9   For their interest in Venetian eighteenth-century furniture etc. see William Odom, *A History of Italian Furniture* (New York 1918, reprint 1967 with an Introduction by Hugh Honour).

10   James was entranced by the eighteenth-century interiors of Palazzo Barbaro and was also attracted, perhaps frivolously he admitted, by Pietro Longhi's anecdotic genre scenes; but he drew the line at the "costly, curly ugliness" of the "rococo church of the Scalzi … all a cold, hard glitter."

11   Evan Charteris op. cit. p.171.

THE SPELL OF THE ENCHANTRESS

1   New York edition (vol III p.vi).

2   *Edel Letters* (vol IV pp.426-431).

3   Helmut and Alison Gernsheim (eds.), *Alvin Langdon Coburn Photographer, an Autobiography* (London 1966 p.54).

4   Ralph F. Bogardus, *Pictures and Texts* (Ann Arbor 1984 p.17).

5   Leon Edel, *Henry James, The Master* (London 1972 p.354).

6   *Edel Letters* (vol IV p.451).

ILLUSTRATIONS

Numerals in the lists of illustrations refer to page numbers.

1879-80. Pastel on brown paper, 30 x 25 cm. Copyright the Frick Collection, New York

46 James Abbott McNeill Whistler, *Upright Venice*, 1879-80. Etching and drypoint, 34 x 17.8 cm. Courtesy of the Coe Gallery

47 James Abbott McNeill Whistler, *The Beggars*, 1879-80. Etching and drypoint, 30.5 x 21 cm. Hunterian Art Gallery, University of Glasgow (Birnie Philip Bequest)

49 James Abbott McNeill Whistler, *The Lagoon, Venice: Nocturne in Blue and Silver*, 1879-80. Canvas, 50.8 x 65.4 cm. Museum of Fine Arts, Boston. Emily L. Ainsley Fund

50 James Abbott McNeill Whistler, *San Giovanni Apostolo et Evangelistae*, 1879-80. Crayon and pastel on grey paper, 30 x 20.2 cm. Freer Gallery of Art, Smithsonian Institution, Washington D.C.

51 James Abbott McNeill Whistler, *Note in Flesh Colour: The Giudecca*, 1879-80. Pastel on paper, 12.7 x 22.8 cm. Mead Art Museum, Amherst (Gift of George D.Pratt, 1893)

52 *Whistler's Wenice*. From *Punch* 12th February 1881

54 James Abbott McNeill Whistler, *Nocturne: San Giorgio*, 1879-80. Chalk and pastel on grey paper, 20.4 x 30 cm. Smithsonian Institution, Freer Gallery of Art, Washington D.C.

55 above John Singer Sargent, *Ralph Curtis on the beach at Scheveningen*, 1880. Oil on board, 27.9 x 3 5.6 cm. The High Museum of Art, Atlanta (Gift of the Walter Clay Hill and Family Foundation)

55 below Anonymous, *John Singer Sargent*, c.1880-85. Ormond Collection

56 above John Singer Sargent, *Mrs Daniel Sargent Curtis*, 1882. Canvas, 71.1 x 53.3 cm. Helen Foresman Spencer Museum of Art, University of Kansas, Lawrence; Samuel H. Kress Study Collection (Photo by Jon Blumb)

56 below John Singer Sargent, *Ramón Subercaseaux*, 1880. Canvas, 47 x 63.5 cm. Private Collection

57 John Singer Sargent, *Venise par temps gris*, 1880-81. Canvas, 50.8 x 71 cm. Private Collection

58 Pierre Auguste Renoir, *Fog in Venice*, 1881. Canvas, 43.8 x 62 cm. Private Collection

60 John Singer Sargent, *Canal Scene (Ponte Panada, Fondamenta Nuove) Venice*, 1880. Watercolour, 25.1 x 35.6 cm. In the collection of the Corcoran Gallery of Art, Washington D.C. (Bequest of Mrs Mabel Stevens Smithers 1952)

60 John Singer Sargent, *Venice*, c.1880-81. Watercolour, 25 x 35.5 cm. The Metropolitan Museum of Art, New York (Gift of Mrs Francis Ormond, 1950)

61 John Singer Sargent, *A Street in Venice*, 1882. Canvas, 45.7 x 52 cm. Courtesy of the Coe Kerr Gallery

62 above John Singer Sargent, *Campo behind the Scuola di San Rocco, Venice*, c.1880-82. Canvas, 66 x 64.8 cm. Private Collection

62 below John Singer Sargent, *A Street in Venice*, 1882. Canvas, 70 x 52.4 cm. Sterling and Francine Clark Institute, Williamstown, Massachusetts

63 John Singer Sargent, *Café on the Riva degli Schiavoni*, c.1881. Watercolour, 24.2 x 34.2 cm. Private Collection. Courtesy of the Coe Kerr Gallery

64 John Singer Sargent, *A Venetian Interior*, c.1880-81. Watercolour, 50.8 x 35.5 cm. Courtesy of the Coe Kerr Gallery

65 John Singer Sargent, *Venetian Women in Palazzo Rezzonico*, c.1880. Canvas, 45.1 x 63.5 cm. Private Collection

66 John Singer Sargent, *Venetian Glass Workers*, c.1880-82. Canvas, 68.0 x 83.1 cm. The Art Institute of Chicago, Mr and Mrs Martin A. Ryerson Collection 1933. 1217

67 Anonymous, *Henry James*, c.1880-85. Lamb House, Rye. Courtesy of the National Trust

68 James Abbott McNeill Whistler, *San Biagio*, 1879-80. Etching and drypoint, 20.6 x 30.5 cm. Courtesy of the Coe Kerr Gallery

69 James Abbott McNeill Whistler, *The Two Doorways*, 1879-80. Etching and drypoint, 20.3 x 29.2 cm. Hunterian Art Gallery, University of Glasgow (Birnie Philip Bequest)

70 above John Singer Sargent, *Venice*, c.1880-81. Watercolour, 25 x 35.5 cm. The Metropolitan Museum of Art, New York (Gift of Mrs Francis Ormond, 1950)

70 below John Singer Sargent, *Venetian Interior*, c.1882. Watercolour, 25.4 x 35.5 cm. Philadelphia Museum of Art

71 left James Abbott McNeill Whistler, *Bead Stringers*, 1879-80. Crayon and pastel on golden brown paper, 27.6 x 11.7 cm. Smithsonian Institution, Freer Gallery of Art, Washington D.C.

71 right Timothy Cole, *Henry James*, 1882. Wood engraving. *Century Magazine*, November 1882

72 left Naya Studio, *Bead Workers*, c.1880. Gelatin print. Böhm Collection, Venice

72 right James Craig Annan, *Campo S. Margherita*, 1896. Photogravure, 14.9 x 5 cm. Royal Photographic Society, Bath

73 John Singer Sargent, *Venetian Water Carriers*, c.1882. Canvas, 64.4 x 70.5 cm. Worcester Art Museum, Worcester, Massachusetts

74 James Craig Annan, *A Beggar*, 1896. Photogravure, 11.5 x 6.9 cm. Royal Photographic Society, Bath

76 Naya studio, *Rio Marin*, c.1890. Silver gelatin print. Böhm Collection, Venice

78 John Singer Sargent, *Venetian Interior*, c.1882. Canvas, 68.3 x 86.8 cm. The Carnegie Museum of Art, Pittsburgh; Purchase 1920

80 James Abbott McNeill Whistler, *The Riva, Sunset. Red and Gold*, 1879-80. Pastel on brown paper, 14 x 26.7 cm. Yale University Art Gallery, Newhaven (Mary Gertrude Abbey Fund)

81 James Abbott McNeill Whistler, *Nocturne: Palaces*, from the Second Venice Set, 1879-80. Etching and drypoint, printed with plate tone on old laid paper, 29.6 x 20.1 cm. Art Gallery of Ontario, Toronto (Gift of Esther and Arthur Gelber, 1982)

82 left Anonymous, *Robert and Pen Browning*, Venice, 1889. British Museum

82 right Anders Zorn, *Isabella Stewart Gardner*, 1894. Canvas, 91 x 66 cm. Isabella Stewart Gardner Museum, Boston

83 right above Anonymous, *Mrs Gardner and a gondolier*, c.1894. Isabella Stewart Gardner Museum, Boston

83 right below Anonymous, *Mrs Gardner, Gaillard Lapsley and a gondolier*, c.1894. Isabella Stewart Gardner Museum, Boston

83 left Joseph Lindon Smith, *Cortile of Palazzo Barbaro*, c.1894. Watercolour, 47.5 x 34 cm. Isabella Stewart Gardner Museum, Boston

84 above Anonymous, *The Gardners and the Zorns*, Venice, 1894. Isabella Stewart Gardner Museum, Boston

84 below Osvaldo Böhm Studio, *The Salone, Palazzo Barbaro*, c.1900

85 above Osvaldo Böhm Studio, *The Library, Palazzo Barbaro*, c.1900

85 below Anonymous, *Henry James's bed in the library, Palazzo Barbaro*, 1892. Isabella Stewart Gardner Museum, Boston

86 James Abbott McNeill Whistler, *Little Venice*, 1879-80. Etching, 18.6 x 26.7 cm. Hunterian Art Gallery, University of Glasgow (Birnie Philip Bequest)

91 James Abbott McNeill Whistler, *Nocturne*, from the First Venice Set, 1879-80. Etching and drypoint, printed in warm brown ink with flat tone on old laid paper, 24 x 29.5 cm. Art Gallery of Ontario, Toronto (Gift of Touche-Ross, 1978)

92 Naya studio, *San Trovaso*, c.1880. Silver gelatin print. Böhm Collection, Venice

93 James Abbott McNeill Whistler, *Bead-Stringing, Venice*, 1879-80. Pastel on brown paper, 29.8 x 19 cm. The Metropolitan Museum of Art, New York (Harris Brisbane Dick Fund 1917)

94 John Singer Sargent, *Street in Venice*, 1882. Panel, 45.1 x 54 cm. National Gallery of Art, Washington D.C. (Avalon Foundation)

97 James Abbott McNeill Whistler, *The Piazzetta*, 1879-80. Etching, 25.4 x 18 cm. Courtesy of the Coe Kerr Gallery

98 John Singer Sargent, *The Pavement, Venice*, 1898. Canvas, 53.3 x 72.4 cm. Private Collection. Courtesy of the Coe Kerr Gallery

99 James Abbott McNeill Whistler, *San Giorgio*, 1879-80. Pastel on brown paper, 19.7 x 29.6 cm. In the collection of the Corcoran Gallery of Art, Washington D.C. (Bequest of James Parmelee)

100 James Abbott McNeill Whistler, *Canal, San Canciano, Venice*, 1879-80. Pastel on brown paper, 28.2 x 18.4 cm. Westmorland Museum of Art, Greensburg, Pennsylvania

102 John Singer Sargent, *Campo dei Frari, Venice*, c.1880-81. Watercolour and gouache, 25.1 x 35.6 cm. In the collection of the Corcoran Gallery of Art, Washington D.C. (Bequest of Mrs Mabel Stevens Smithers 1952)

102 Ralph Curtis, *The Gondola*, 1884. Canvas, 74 x 142 cm. Isabella Stewart Gardner Museum, Boston

103 James Abbott McNeill Whistler, *The Traghetto*, No.2, 1879-80. Etching and drypoint, 23.5 x 30.5 cm. Courtesy of the Coe Kerr Gallery

105 John Singer Sargent, *Sortie de l'église*, 1880-82. Ink on paper, 19 x 30.5 cm. Private Collection

106 John Singer Sargent, *Campo S. Agnese, Venice*, 1890. Canvas, 45.7 x 52.7 cm. Wellesley College Museum, Collection of the Gift of Strafford Morse in memory of his wife, Gabrielle Ladd Morse (Class of 1959), Wellesley

108 John Singer Sargent, *Interior of the Doges' Palace, Venice*, 1898. Canvas, 49.5 x 79 cm. Collection of the Earl of Harewood

111 above Carlo Naya, *Chioggia*, c.1890. Silver gelatin print. Böhm Collection, Venice

111 below Naya Studio, *Lido landing-stage*, c.1990. Silver gelatin print. Böhm Collection, Venice

112 James Abbott McNeill Whistler, *The Little Lagoon*, 1879-80 Etching, 22.6 x 15.2 cm. Hunterian Art Gallery, University of Glasgow (Birnie Philip Bequest)

113 James Abbott McNeill Whistler, *The Isles of Venice*, 1879-80. Pastel on brown paper, 9.4 x 28.5 cm. Smithsonian Institute, Freer Gallery of Art, Washington D.C.

114 John Singer Sargent, *Venice*, c.1902. Watercolour, 25.2 x 35.4 cm. Worcester Art Museum, Worcester, Massachusetts (Gift of Mr and Mrs Stuart Riley Jr.)

115 John Singer Sargent, *S. Maria della Salute, Venice*, c.1903. Watercolour, 34.9 x 53.5 cm. Isabella Stewart Gardner Museum, Boston

116 left John Singer Sargent, *The Salute, Venice*, c.1903. Watercolour over pencil on paper, 50.8 x 35.6 cm. Yale University Art Gallery, Christian A. Zabriskie Fund. Newhaven, Connecticut

116 right John Singer Sargent, *Venice: La Dogana*, c.1911. Watercolour, 50 x 36 cm. Museum of Fine Arts, Boston (Charles Henry Hayden Fund)

119 John Singer Sargent, *Doorway of a Venetian Palace*, c.1905-10. Watercolour, 58.4 x 45.7 cm. Westmorland Museum of Art, Greensburg, Pennsylvania

120 Giovanni Battista Brusa, *Regatta Day, Venice*, 1891. Royal Photographic Society, Bath

121 John Singer Sargent, *Festa della Regatta*, c.1903 Watercolour on paper and oil on glass, 34 x 49.5 cm. Courtesy of the Coe Kerr Gallery

123 John Singer Sargent, *The Grand Canal, Venice*, c.1905-10. Watercolour, 35.5 x 50.8 cm. Courtesy of the Coe Kerr Gallery

126 John Singer Sargent, *Gondoliers' Siesta*, 1905. Watercolour, 25.2 x 50.4 cm. Collection of Mr and Mrs Raymond J. Horowitz

128 John Singer Sargent, *Venetian Doorway*, c.1900. Watercolour, 54.6 x 37.1 cm. The Metropolitan Museum of Art, New York (Gift of Mrs Francis Ormond, 1950)

129 John Singer Sargent, *Palazzo Labia with the Campanile of San Geremia*, 1906. Watercolour, 36 x 25 cm. Courtesy of the Coe Kerr Gallery

133 John Singer Sargent, *S. Giuseppe di Castello*, Venice, c.1903-4. Watercolour, 30.6 x 45.8 cm. Isabella Stewart Gardner Museum, Boston

134 John Singer Sargent, *Ponte della Canonica, Venice,* c.1903-4. Watercolour, 45.8 x 30.6 cm. Isabella Stewart Gardner Museum, Boston

136 John Singer Sargent, *Rio di San Salvatore, Venice,* c.1903-4. Watercolour, 25.1 x 35.5 cm. Isabella Stewart Gardner Museum, Boston

138 left Ludwig Johann Passini, *Katherine De Kay Bronson,* 1890. Watercolour, 45x30cm. Private Collection

138 right Ludwig Johann Passini, *Edith Bronson,* 1890. Watercolour, 28 x 20 cm. Private Collection

139 Anonymous, *Interior of Ca' Alvisi,* c.1890. Private Collection

140 Anonymous, *Mrs Bronson's household servants at Ca' Alvisi,* 1888. Courtesy of the Browning Institute

141 Anonymous, *Ca' Alvisi, Venice,* 1888. Canvas, 30.5 x 20 cm. Private Collection

146 John Singer Sargent, *An Interior in Venice,* 1899. Canvas, 64.8 x 80.7 cm. Royal Academy, London

149 Anonymous photograph of Ludwig Johann Passini's *Portrait of Isabella Stewart Gardner,* Venice, 1892, present whereabouts of painting unknown

152 John Singer Sargent, *Henry James,* 1913. Canvas, 84.6 x 68.4 cm. National Portrait Gallery, London

153 Anonymous photograph of Mrs Daniel Curtis and Ralph Curtis in the Salone of Palazzo Barbaro, c.1910. Isabella Stewart Gardner Museum, Boston

154 John Singer Sargent, *Rococo Mirror,* 1898. Canvas, 58.3 x 45.7 cm. Courtesy of the Coe Kerr Gallery

155 John Singer Sargent, *Sketching on the Giudecca,* c.1904. Watercolour and gouache, 35.6 x 52.7 cm. Private Collection

156 top John Singer Sargent, *The Rialto,* Venice, c.1911. Canvas, 55.9 x 91.5 cm. Philadelphia Museum of Art (The George W. Elkins Collection)

156 bottom Anonymous photograph of Emily Sargent and Eliza Wedgwood, Venice, c.1911. Ormond Collection

157 top right John Singer Sargent, *The Libreria,* Venice, 1904. Watercolour, 51 x 36 cm. Private collection

157 bottom John Singer Sargent, *A Venetian Canal,* c.1910. Watercolour, 39.2 x 63 cm. The Metropolitan Museum of Art, New York (Joseph Pulitzer Bequest 1915)

158 Claude Monet, *Santa Maria della Salute,* 1908-12. Canvas, 72 x 92 cm. Private Collection

160 Muster-Böhm photograph, *Ponte dell'Accademia,* c.1910. Böhm Collection, Venice

161 Alvin Langdon Coburn, Frontispiece for *The Wings of the Dove,* 1906 (New York edition of *The Novels and Tales of Henry James,* London 1909)

162 Alvin Langdon Coburn, Frontispiece for *The Aspern Papers,* 1906 (New York edition of *The Novels and Tales of Henry James,* 1913)

163 Alvin Langdon Coburn, *The White Bridge,* 1906. Platinum and gum print. Courtesy Christie's, London

INDEX

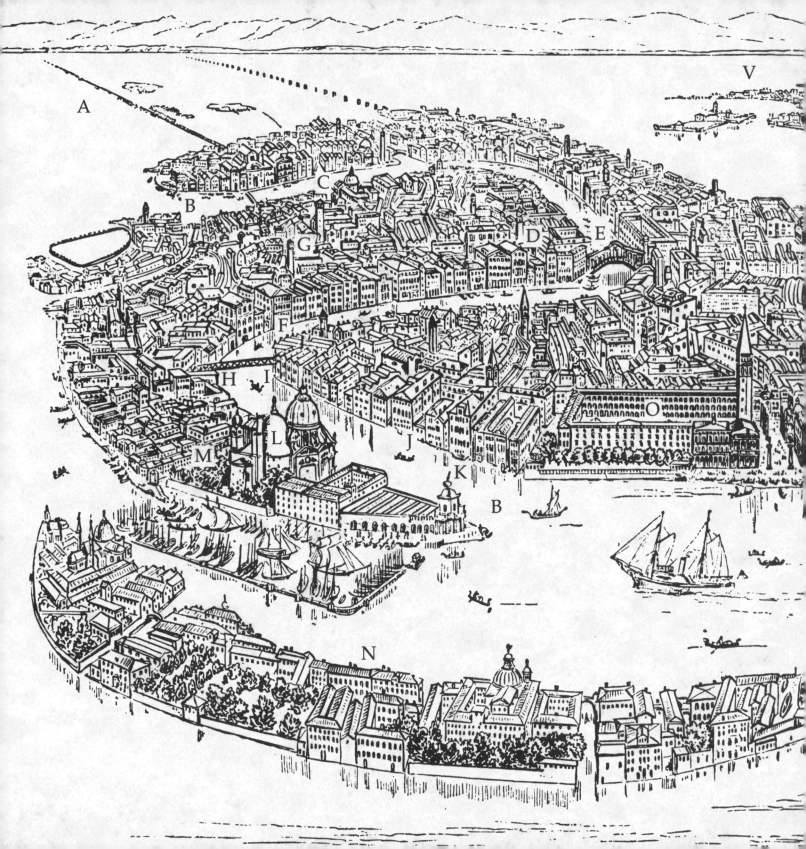